common sense ministry

common sense ministry

A
BLUEPRINT FOR
SUCCESSFUL
LAITY AND PASTORAL
LEADERSHIP

James A. Cress

Ministerial Association Resource Center
General Conference of Seventh-day Adventists

Dedication

This book is dedicated to my spouse

Sharon M. Cress

in appreciation for her partnership in marriage, in acknowledgement of her service to pastoral families, and in affirmation of her call to ministry.

Edited by John M. Fowler

Cover design by Harry Knox

Copyright © 1999 by
Ministerial Association Resource Center
General Conference of Seventh-day Adventists
12501 Old Columbia Pike, Silver Spring, MD 20904
(301) 680-6508

Printed in the United States of America by
Pacific Press Publishing Association
Nampa, Idaho
All Rights Reserved

ISBN 1-57847-059-5

BUSIER THAN JESUS

A ll pastors are busy. I was busier than Jesus. Now, don't castigate me for blasphemous presumption: how could I be busier than the Creator of the universe? I am not the only one who has found himself or herself overextended—busier than Jesus. And before you finish reading this you too may find yourself busier than Jesus.

One thing I have discovered is how easy it is to confuse the urgent with the important. For example, in my pastorate I found that my time was more easily consumed putting out fires than lighting them in the hearts of my people or even in my own heart. Unless intentionally protected, my agenda became so filled with doing good that I failed to do right.

If you couple this reality with a work-ethic model that values activity as a measure of productivity, one thing becomes predestined: "doing" will receive more emphasis than "being." Which, of course, is the crux of the issue. To the extent that my time for personal devotions and spiritual growth gave way to the demands of the urgent, I became busier than Jesus.

Not that Jesus wasn't busy. In fact, when my life is most crowded with crisis and urgent demands, I am just beginning to sense what it must have been to have the people of Palestine constantly crowding Jesus for what they knew He could give them. How easy it would have been for Him to rely on "doing" good more than "being." "In a life wholly devoted to the good of others, the Saviour found it necessary to . . . turn aside from a life of ceaseless activity and contact with human needs, to seek retirement and unbroken communion with His Father."[1]

[1]Ellen G. White, *The Desire of Ages* (Mountain View, Calif.: Pacific Press Publishing Association, 1940), pp. 362, 363.

Pastoral overextension is first noted and its negative impact first felt in the pastor's marriage and home, well before most church members perceive its presence. This is because we can mask our lives more easily before those with whom we meet and worship for only a few hours weekly than before those with whom we live daily. If I don't pray this week, few of my members may immediately know. But if I don't pray today, my spouse, children, and even my dog will probably feel it tomorrow!

Furthermore, if I want to effect spiritual change in my members, the place to start is in myself. The old adage still holds true—spirituality of members will not grow beyond that of their leaders. In our congregation we tried an intentional yearlong experiment to increase our corporate spirituality. We did this by looking at the roots of spiritual growth—Bible study, prayer, fellowship, witnessing, and obedience. Each one of us looked at the issues in a personal way. My own prayer and study life improved as I admonished my members to progress in these areas. My motive of modeling for them challenged my own spiritual growth.

For twelve months we continued our study and prayer, encouraged increased fellowship and witness, and reflected on personal obedience to Jesus. We added five more minutes to whatever time we were spending in personal spiritual growth activities. At the end of the year we measured our progress by a congregational survey. Eighty-six percent indicated that they were now more obedient to God's will for their personal lives than they were a year earlier. The methods were simple; the results momentous.

If you find yourself busier than Jesus, I encourage you to experimentally investigate your priorities. Do a self-analysis of the urgent and the important, the doing and the being. Discover for yourself that personal spirituality increases as you focus on being about your Saviour's business.

EVALUATION:
WHOSE OPINION COUNTS?

H ow am I doing?" Everywhere he went Ed Koch would question his constituents. As a politician, the former mayor of New York City wanted instant feedback from the people who mattered most—the ones who would vote for him.

Pastors also need feedback from the people who matter most—the ones who vote with their attendance, financial support, and ministering activities.

However, there are few jobs in which it is harder to measure progress or to get accurate feedback than pastoral ministry.

Furthermore, one of the least reliable methods of seeking realistic input is to ask some parishioners, "How am I doing?" Depending upon whose input you seek, the answers will vary. You are seldom as great as your strongest supporters will affirm, and you are seldom as bad as your loudest detractors will decry.

If we surround ourselves only with those who affirm our ministry, we may not get accurate evaluation. Likewise, if naysayers are the only voices we hear, it is easy to become discouraged or to conclude that we are ineffective. So whose opinions count?

What is God's opinion?

Pastors must first seek to place their lives and ministry in harmony with God's will and to maintain a keen sense of His approval! Determine that you will follow His lead. Henrietta Mears says, "To be successful in God's work is to fall in line with His will and to do it His way. All that is pleasing to Him will be a success."

What do your administrative leaders say?

After making sure of your compliance with God's will, seek the counsel of your administrators. One of the best pieces of advice I received as a young pastor was, "If you wonder how to proceed in any situation, call your president." This doesn't mean that administrators are perfect or always have the best solutions. But it does mean that if you seek and follow their counsel, they can and will support you. Try never to place your supervisors in the position of hearing about difficult matters that you have failed to discuss with them.

Are local leaders with you?

Trusting the elected leadership of the congregation is essential for pastoral effectiveness just as trust for the pastor by laity leadership is essential for effective church growth. More often than not, elders and church officers are selected because the congregation values their leadership and trusts their judgment. Wise pastors will recognize that their pastoral tenure will eventually conclude while their members will live with decisions far into the future.

Consult with your leaders and then motivate them to act upon the decisions they have made. Some of the most delicate issues are best resolved when local church leaders have participated in decision-making and then are expected to implement the course of action that they have designed.

Members vote regularly

A pastor must have vision and set the pace. Your church will seldom exceed your expectations for what they can accomplish, so set a higher standard for soulwinning, financial goals, attendance, and spirituality. Encourage your members to reach beyond what they think they can do. Measurable progress will follow as you raise their vision of what can be accomplished. This process will help raise your own sights.

Your spouse has loving wisdom

Don't ignore the input of your partner in marriage and ministry. Sometimes in the stress of too-busy schedules and too-long days, a spouse's evaluation can sound like criticism and might be discarded as nagging. Take time to listen to the message your family members give. They love you and want to see your ministry succeed. Initiate opportunities to spend a quiet evening with your partner reflecting on the course of your ministry. You will receive profound insights that will benefit you immensely.

Find a friend

A trusted pastoral colleague knows the burdens you carry and shares the same kinds of challenges you face. A friend often sees your point of view but is able to maintain a "one-step-away" objectivity that places even the most difficult matters in a different perspective.

Whom to ignore

While every member deserves a voice, remember that some individuals thrive on recreational griping. Chronic complainers believe they have failed to do their duty until they find fault. Nothing you do will please them, and accommodations you make to their complaints will seldom earn their support.

Such sideline umpires are typically uninvolved in church programs or evangelistic endeavors. Carefully evaluate your own attitudes but recognize that a murmuring multitude has always dogged the steps of spiritual leaders.

Focus on finding God's will and building your leaders' support and then move forward in confidence.

THE MANY FACES OF POWER

"All power is given unto me in heaven and in earth."
— Matthew 28:18

S ince Jesus first uttered those words, His followers have tried to appropriate some of this power for themselves. Jesus' own disciples constantly bickered about who would be the greatest and who would achieve the most prominent positions in the kingdom they were convinced He was about to establish.

Today we are no less fascinated than those disciples by the attainment and use of power. It is important for us, as pastors and elders called to lead God's people, to understand the proper use of power, as well as to learn to avoid its abuse.

Ted Engstrom, in the introduction to his book *The Making of a Christian Leader,* says, "Solid, dependable, loyal, strong leadership is one of the most desperate needs in America and in our world today. We see the tragedy of weak men in important places—little men in big jobs. . . .

"When we decry the scarcity of leadership talent in our society, we are not talking about a lack of people to fill administrative or executive positions. . . .

"What we are deeply concerned about is a scarcity of those people who are willing to assume significant leadership roles in our society to get the job done effectively. The effective leader doesn't wait for things to happen, he helps make things happen. He takes the initiative."[1]

Engstrom goes on to define a leader as "one who guides and develops the activities of others and seeks to provide continual training and direction."[2] By so defining leaders, Engstrom gets directly to the issue of power and pastoral leadership. Pastoral power must be focused on the objective of discerning and developing the ministry of the laity in a non-manipulative way.

This involves recruitment and training and releases those you mentor to utilize their training in real-life situations. Pastors should be accountable, both to those who supervise their work and to those whom they serve, for duplicating their capabilities in the lives of their members. Leaders must train other leaders. In short, the work of the pastor is to work the members.

Sometimes clergy misunderstand and misappropriate power. Usually this is not done from a malevolent motive but from an insufficient comprehension of the various sources and the responsible use of power. What are some of these faces of power?

Position power comes by virtue of the office or position held. By being elected or appointed, the leader receives designated power from the job itself. This power immediately transfers to the individual who is next elected.

Information power comes by virtue of knowledge or skills that the leader possesses. This power is retained as long as the information is necessary to the group's continued well-being.

Reward power comes by virtue of rewards or perks that the leader can grant or withhold. Often reward power, like all carrot-and-stick motivation, tends to be viewed as either paternalistic or manipulative even when the rewarder does not intend to utilize it wrongfully.

Relational power comes to individuals by association with those who hold power. Such individuals may be referred to as the "inner circle." Such power tends to evaporate quickly following a change in association or the removal of the leader. Relational power is most stable when it involves a good working relationship between team members.

Personal power is derived by the confidence which others place in a leader's moral integrity, skills, reputation, and past accomplishments. Stronger than other power sources, personal power does not evaporate with a change in status or circumstances. Instead, such changes usually enhance personal power as the individual responds creatively and appropriately to the new situation.

Jesus is history's most outstanding example of One who held the highest of all positions, who was omniscient, who enjoyed the most intimate association with the heavenly Father and the Holy Spirit. Yet, despite all of that, He willingly emptied Himself of all these sources of power and came to this earth as a servant-leader whose ministry was the essence of personal power.

As we strive more to exercise His power in our ministry than to appropriate His power for our own use, the Holy Spirit can grant us an abundance of that which Jesus promised: "Ye shall receive power" (Acts 1:8).

[1] Ted W. Engstrom, *The Making of a Christian Leader* (Grand Rapids: Zondervan Publishing House, 1976), introduction.

[2] Ibid.

SEXUAL MISCONDUCT:
A CALL TO CONSISTENCY

Like ripples from a rock dropped into a quiet pool, the trauma of clergy sexual misconduct spreads well beyond the personal life of those directly involved.

The toll, of course, is heavy for the one who has abused a position of trust—loss of relationship with family and parishioners, loss of respect, loss of leadership, loss of employment, and loss of church membership.

But the trauma goes beyond the pastor's personal loss. The pastor's spouse and children feel branded by a sin in which they did not participate. Congregational, organizational, and even collegial support structures that minister to others in crisis now appear to abandon the pastoral family.

Victims of abuse also suffer. Clearly these individuals are victims, whether they believe they have freely chosen the illicit relationship or not. Sexual misconduct by professionals, such as physicians, attorneys, therapists, teachers, and clergy, who hold power or authority over their victims, amounts to a betrayal of trust and an exploitation of the victim, jeopardizing the victim's home, family, and status in the community of believers.

The reputation of the congregation is also damaged, and its members' ability to trust future leaders is stymied. Typically, it takes more than a decade for a congregation to recover from the trauma of pastoral sexual misconduct.

Ministerial colleagues and the wider body of the denomination also suffer from lowered esteem for spiritual leaders and a generalized assumption that "all clergy are like that!"

Ultimately, Christianity in general suffers public scorn from those who mock the sins of those who have been granted spiritual trust.

No wonder the penalty, historically, has been severe for pastors who morally fall. Increased responsibility means greater accountability. Parishioners have a right to expect the best from their pastors and to believe that a leadership position should not be a launching pad for sexual abuse of power.

Inconsistency in discipline

Increasingly, however, we find sexual misconduct covered up, ignored, or treated as a minor infraction, leaving the guilty clergy free for reappointment to another pastoral role, often without so much as a lapse in service.

Recent cases include clergy who have been "disciplined" for a moral fall and yet reassigned pastoral duties within the same month.

One conference requested a congregation to apply church discipline to its morally fallen pastor while administrators continued to maintain his ministerial credentials that enabled him to enter a clinical pastoral education (CPE) course to prepare for chaplaincy ministry. The church refused to discipline a pastor who was still credentialed by the conference.

Such examples are too typical. They directly violate church policy which states: *"It is recognized that a minister who has experienced a moral fall or has apostatized has access to the mercy and pardoning grace of God and may desire to return to the church. Such an individual must be assured of the love and goodwill of his brethren. However, for the sake of the good name of the church and the maintaining of moral standards, he must plan to devote his life to employment other than that of the gospel ministry, the teaching ministry, or denominational leadership."*[1]

Policy does not equivocate. *"He shall be ineligible for future employment as a Seventh-day Adventist minister."*[2]

Reinstalling or quietly transferring a morally lapsed clergy hurts the body of Christ. Church members, on the one hand, are scandalized and may assume that the church administration colludes to protect its own. Members may thus conclude that what is acceptable for leadership should be applicable to them, and violate the seventh commandment with impunity.

Likewise, the church faces enormous legal risk continuing a person in employment after knowing that such an individual has indulged in sexual abuse of power.

If current policy needs revision to allow for employment restoration of clergy involved in sexual misconduct, an appropriate process exists for debating and amending policy. Every viewpoint can be discussed and evaluated. In the meantime administrators should not establish precedents that are scofflaws or continue to disregard policy under the rubric of compassion.

Of course fallen pastors need compassion. But forgiveness and compassion do not guarantee job security. Compassion should focus more on spiritual restoration than on continuation of employment. While I might personally rejoice for individuals who have found professional restoration, I grieve for the increasing perception which concludes that a well-connected or popular clergy who has engaged in professional sexual misconduct will professionally survive while others, less well connected, will be terminated without recourse.

Further, it is helpful to note that current policy envisions compassion along with discipline: *"Where practical, the organization involved should provide a professional program of counseling and career guidance for the minister and family to assist them in transition."*[3]

Compassion and discipline

Several years ago the General Conference Ministerial Association prepared the following resolution:

"Whereas the call to ministry is a sacred trust, involving among other things a respect for the personhood of people as envisioned in the seventh commandment, and any breach of trust in this area brings reproach to ministry, to the church, and to God;

"Whereas it is unreasonable to ask members to trust pastors who have engaged in sexual misconduct (adultery, pedophilia, homosexuality, fornication, etc.);

"Whereas the church is at legal risk when employing or transferring as pastors, teachers, or administrators those with a history of sexual misconduct;

"Whereas the conference is the ordaining and employing authority of the church, and is charged with the sacred responsibility of protecting, preserving, and projecting the good name of the church, and maintaining standards in the ministry for the glory of God;

"Whereas confusion exists where no consistent policy is applied, leaving many pastors convinced that it is not what one does but whom one knows that determines the discipline received;

"We strongly recommend that the established policy be followed in both its disciplinary and its redemptive provisions."

Consistency is needed. If current policy needs revision, then let us address the issue in a way that answers questions and avoids charges of cronyism or cover-up. If current policy, disqualifying ministers who have experienced a moral fall from future pastoral or church leadership, is appropriate, then let us stand united in its application rather than allowing some to reenter ministry while excluding others.

Above all, let us emphasize a code of sexual ethics for church-employed professionals that seriously acknowledges that any sexual misconduct within the context of ministry is professionally unethical and morally wrong. Let us also find practical ways to help those who find themselves heading toward such misconduct to seek professional assistance to avoid the moral fall that could destroy their ministry.

[1] *Working Policy of the General Conference of Seventh-day Adventists* (Hagerstown, MD.: Review and Herald Publishing Association, 1992-1993), p. 332 (*italics* supplied).

[2] Ibid., p. 331 (*italics* supplied).

[3] Ibid., p. 332 (*italics* supplied).

CAREFUL!
YOUR SYMBOL IS SHOWING!

What do your symbols say? Christians have always employed meaningful symbols to describe their faith, to identify their understanding of mission, to embrace an ideal, or to rally the faithful to spiritual warfare.

Likewise, Scripture is full of symbols. Think of a few that are used to describe Jesus—a lion from Judah as deliverer, an innocent lamb offered in sacrifice, the rejected cornerstone, the rose of Sharon, the balm of Gilead, or the rock cut without hands that crushes all in its path to victory.

Symbols are not wrong. God Himself employs their communicative ability. "I have given symbols through the witness of the prophets" (Hosea 12:10, NKJV). "And in that day there shall be a Root of Jesse, who shall stand as a banner to the people" (Isaiah 11:10, NKJV).

Sometimes, however, the symbols we use are meaningless or, worse, offensive. Imagine my horror when our Pathfinder club was notified that its flag was offensive because it was similar to a Nazi banner from that tragic era preceding World War II.

"With the cross of Jesus going on before." If in these words you hear the refrain of a great Christian hymn and are reminded of the power of the gospel to advance into all the world, you will find the cross a magnificent symbol of triumph. However, if you were on the receiving end of the great crusades during the Middle Ages, you would view the same cross as an imperialistic symbol of those who wish to force either your conversion or your eradication.

Our *Ministry* editor once recounted a story I had shared of changing the church signboard. Instead of three angels, in an artistic but vague symbolic style, we chose the more familiar emblem of the cross. Our change was intentional. While the angels had portrayed our self-understanding of a unique last-day message, they conveyed no meaning to the community. We wished to state clearly that we were Christians with our ministry centered in the Saviour.

A few days after the new signboard was in place I met an unchurched friend at a business luncheon who remarked that she had noted our new design. Commenting on the clarity of the cross for a Christian organization, she added, "Every time I passed your church before, I wondered what those three bugs were all about." Imagine! We had portrayed angels. She had seen insects.

Do your symbols communicate what you intend?

While those angels held deep meaning to anyone who understood what they were and what they represented, they were meaningless to the uninitiated.

On the other hand, I had little realized how much emotion and energy can be stirred by a simple change in symbols. Certain individuals immediately pounced upon this change to prove that our congregation had abandoned the faith. They declared our cross a compromise that was just the tip of the iceberg on our journey to apostasy.

Even our reminder of the powerful scriptural impact of the cross could not persuade those critics whose fervor was exceeded only by their ignorance. They were not interested in the words of the apostle Paul: *"But God forbid that I should glory except in the cross of our Lord Jesus Christ, by whom the world has been crucified to me and I to the world."* Their minds were made up. They had found their cause. They were disinterested in how the community perceived our "three insects" as long as there was no compromise in "the way we had always done things."

Recently I saw another new church sign where the angels look like three swimmers in competition. At least the church was in Atlanta, host to the 1996 Olympics. Perhaps viewers will conclude that this congregation embraces the spirit of international games!

We should consider what our symbols say. If we use three angels, they may communicate effectively to our members but ineffectively to the world.

We should also consider for whom our symbols are intended. Early Christians used the symbol of the fish to identify each other as believers. But they used the scandalous cross to proclaim the essentials of salvation through Jesus Christ.

Personally, I prefer symbols that are so unambiguous that no one need wonder about either our message or our mission.

WHERE THE ACTION IS

Tip O'Neill, former speaker of the U.S. House of Representatives, said it well: "All politics are local." He meant, of course, that what happens in government is unimportant until it impacts people back home where they live.

The same is true for the church. Effective, life-changing ministry occurs in local congregations, not bureaucratic structures or committee labyrinths.

Not so long ago, our Ministerial Association staff identified issues upon which we ought to focus and the key results to expect. Out of this came a renewed consensus that the local congregation is the site of real ministry. We believe the following thirteen key results can be expected from a proper focus on a local church-based ministry. See how they resonate with your own convictions and ministry priorities.

1. Members experience personal joy of salvation. I believe our people have no greater need than to experience a vibrant, personal relationship with Jesus Christ. Indeed, stronger church life can be summed up in this reality: "He who has the Son has life" (1 John 5:12).*

2. Members experience hope in the reality and nearness of Christ's coming. We are Adventists because of the Advent. The return of Jesus is not only our name; it is our reason for existence. Amid social, economic, and moral chaos, I long for my members to be confident in the blessed hope!

3. Members experience personal Sabbath rest. Far beyond the identification of the correct day of worship, it is essential to experience total rest in Jesus—mind, body, and soul. Resting

securely in a saving relationship with the Lord of the Lord's day is the essence of Sabbath keeping.

4. Members experience joyful family relationships. Love in our marriages and with our families becomes a foretaste of fellowship throughout eternity in Christ's kingdom. Bathed in this blessed hope, members become willing to work through their difficult relationships instead of abandoning commitment. The resulting health of these home-based relationships will attract others to Jesus living in us.

5. Members experience fellowship of all believers together, living a love that transcends barriers of nationality, race, tribe, age, gender, or social status. "By this all men will know that you are my disciples, if you love one another" (John 13:35).

6. Members experience ownership of the church's mission. What a victory if my members see their church as more than just the place to go on Sabbath. Going beyond mere belief in the church's mission, I want them to experience personal investment in mission. This involves their time, their talents, their energy, and their funds.

7. Members receive motivation, empowerment, and equipment for ministry. The work of the pastor is to foster the work of members. I long for pastoral leaders (both clergy and laity elders who serve in ministerial functions) to view as their first task the training of believers into becoming disciples.

8. Members receive permission and encouragement to serve their surrounding community. We have too much isolationistic judgment of society and too little involvement in our neighborhoods. Jesus saw the church as salt and light to the world. So let's get out of the saltshaker and into the world.

9. Members experience success in evangelism. Harvesting souls for the kingdom is the business of every believer, not

just professional evangelists. I long for my members to experience the joy of conversion in people for whom they personally labor. If we wait for the professionals to fulfill the gospel commission, we will wait in our graves. "The harvest is plentiful, but the workers are few. Ask the Lord of the harvest, therefore, to send out workers into his harvest field" (Luke 10:2).

10. Members learn discernment and discretion. Scripture admonishes, "Test everything. Hold on to the good" (1 Thessalonians 5:21). When my members are bombarded by spurious tales and sensational conjectures, I long for discretion that separates every wind of doctrine or devilish rumor from the truth as it is in Jesus.

11. Members teach kingdom values to the coming generation. The purpose of our extensive parochial educational system—a partnership of teachers, parents, and pastors—must be to develop individuals who think God's thoughts and live God's way. Our students learn from our priorities those values in which they will invest their future.

12. Members express confidence in God's leading. As we recall divine providence throughout our history and His continued presence moving us toward the victorious conclusion of the great controversy, we can fearlessly rejoice that "all His biddings are enablings."

13. Members are served by pastors who lead as visionaries of greatness for God, facilitators of deepness in spiritual maturity, and enablers of real-life service to others. This is the pastor I want to be, and it is my prayer that this is the pastoral ministry you will experience.

*Texts are from the New International Version.

LESSONS FROM
A TRAGEDY

Earthquake! If the word sounds ominous, the experience is even more so. At 4:31 a.m., January 17, 1994, Sharon and I were nearly thrown off our hotel bed. During the next few seconds of horror we simultaneously held each other, groped for a light, tried to assimilate what was happening, and prayed aloud for deliverance. At times like that, 35 seconds can feel like a lifetime.

We have always believed earthquakes are a sign of Jesus' coming, but this one seemed like the end of the world itself. Surviving the Los Angeles earthquake remains in our memories long after the "city of angels" has been reconstructed.

In those first moments after the tremors quieted, we rejoiced to be alive and unharmed even as we struggled to replace items that had fallen to the floor and to bring about order out of the chaos surrounding us. Our natural conclusion was to assume that everyone else was as secure as ourselves. Even television stations initially reported that damage was relatively insignificant as they projected their own experience onto the entire community.

Despite ongoing significant aftershocks, the early conclusion was that most of Los Angeles had escaped and little lasting damage had occurred. Only the dawn and the subsequent tragedies brought the real horror to reality—a devastating earthquake had taken another major toll on this metropolitan area that just recently had suffered riots, fires, floods, and landslides, adding to the usual problems of crime and destruction rampant in today's urban society.

Having survived this quake, Sharon and I have learned some significant lessons.

The first viewpoint is usually inaccurate. Our assumption that all had escaped harm was natural as we projected our own experience onto the whole milieu. Our error, of course, was to reduce the total tragedy to our own experience. Because we had no more than the emotional trauma of a "good scare," it was easy to believe that others were just as secure. In retrospect, we realize that we repeat such false assumptions in various circumstances when we measure others only by ourselves and our own limited experience.

There have been earthquakes far more deadly in which thousands have perished. But because this is the worst we had personally survived, it was easy to assign more trauma to this than to any other tragedy. Perhaps that is what the quipster meant who said, "the only exercise some people get is jumping to conclusions."

With the arrival of full information, our analysis changed. Our conclusions formed in fantasy were changed by the reality that others had suffered significant loss and that at least 60 lives ended at the very moment we had been praying for ours to be spared.

Things change. No matter what security we provide for ourselves, no matter what caution we might personally exhibit, forces beyond our control can swiftly alter the best plans. The past few years have demonstrated globally how quickly governments and social structures turn unstable or even vanish. How correct is the observation that earth's final movements will be rapid!

Priorities change. If I were asked to calmly analyze what I might take from my home if I were forced to leave, what I might select would be far different than if I were given only moments to flee a home that was collapsing about me. I will long remember the anguished mother who said all she really wanted from her destroyed home were photographs of her children and mementos of her marriage.

Emergencies bring out the best (and worst) in people. Los Angeles abounded with thousands of individuals who saw a need and did something about it. Naturally, government and organized relief agencies, including Adventist Development and Relief Agency (ADRA), moved quickly to bring aid.

But help also came from individuals. From those who opened their homes to shelter others to those who rescued disoriented pets, the city's trauma was met by the quiet heroics of ordinary people who understood that they could not change the world but recognized that they could make a difference one person at a time.

Not everyone was helpful. Hundreds took advantage of the tragedy, gouged the prices of basic supplies, or looted the remains of businesses and homes. We still live in a world of sin, and, until Jesus restores all things, other crises will reveal those who care only for themselves. Innocents will still suffer the most. That is the tragic reality of sin.

Others face greater disasters than me. Despite returning home to face savage cold and a day in the emergency hospital from falling on ice, I still was blessed compared with those who lost everything.

My challenges are minor compared to theirs. My privilege is to recognize their need and to employ my resources to bring beneficial change, one person at a time!

KEEPING WHAT
WE REAP

If we build it, will they come? If they come, will they stay? If they stay, will we run them off? As Adventists prepared to launch NET '98, another evangelistic thrust via satellite downlink and our greatest such project in history, the questions were obviously on target.

NET '98 was similar in many ways to evangelistic meetings you may have conducted or observed in the past. It took place in a local church. A pastor, rather than visiting evangelist, presented the messages. Members of the local congregations attended and invited their friends. Good news from God's Word was proclaimed, and, by the Spirit's power, people became disciples of Jesus Christ.

In other ways, however, NET '98 was far from typical. For starters, thousands of congregations and hundreds of thousands of people on six continents participated in the same event as it was translated into some forty languages.

Generation X was the target. The defining characteristic, the thing that most set it apart from past evangelistic endeavors, is that NET '98 intentionally targeted young adults, ages 18-33, often referred to as Generation X (GenX).

Anticipating what would happen, host pastor Dwight Nelson said, "What we share together is going to be life-changing for all ages. We are going to be user-friendly for the young."[1]

It was no accident that NET '98 originated from a campus congregation surrounded by some three thousand young adults.[2]

This primary purpose was clearly articulated in a *Adventist Review* interview: "NET '98 is going to reach GenXers."[3]

As Dwight Nelson correctly analyzed, if young adults accounted for more than one in eight of the baptisms attributed to the earlier NET '96, an event attended mainly by people over fifty years of age, we have good reason to believe that many more young GenXers will respond to these messages which have been developed with them specifically in mind.

The challenge, of course, was that GenXers are quite different from the older generations who, historically, have been the greatest supporters of evangelistic projects.

Seeking practical ways to conserve the new members, especially GenXers, who would embrace the Adventist message in response to NET '98, I asked a number of colleagues to help me answer the big question: How do you make young people feel welcome in your congregation when you are not sure you even like them?[4]

The crucial question. Therefore, the urgent question for Adventist congregations around the world was: "How will we keep those we reap?" Recent statistics indicate that we have plenty of room to grow in assimilating any new members, but especially young adult members. How can we close the "back doors" of our churches through which too may depart?

Congregations that will respond best to the challenge of keeping GenXers in the church are those that exhibit a readiness to learn, grow, and change.

Characteristics of GenXers. Learning what makes GenXers tick can be an exciting adventure for pastors and congregations and provide a basis for integrating these young people into our congregations. Current research tells us that:

• There are lots of them. Forty-six million people were born in the United States between 1965-1980.

• They are a diverse group with characteristics in common with several billion of their peers worldwide.

• They don't like labels. When we refer to them as Generation X, Baby Busters, or twenty-somethings, they view such terms as an older generation's attempts to impose a label or put them in a box. "I am not a target market," protests a young adult in Douglas Coupland's novel, *Generation X.* "Why can't I just be a person? And why can't we relate together as people?"[5]

• They often feel alone, abandoned, and alienated. Aloneness occurs in the midst of people when a young adult feels unable to connect with others in deeply fulfilling ways. Nearly half of young adults are children of divorce. Many wrestle with abandonment issues. It's hard to get close because they don't want you to hurt them the same way their families have hurt them. They feel alienated and have a deep need to experience reconciliation with others.

• Relationships are important. Many young adults exhibit a deep hunger for community. They feel most alive when they are with their friends and find fulfillment in relationships more than in the traditional accompaniments of success. They may change careers as many as six times during adulthood, often for relational reasons.

• They like to do things in groups. Dating, recreation, and shopping are frequently group activities. "The era of individual has ended. A new era of team and community has arrived."[6]

• There are no absolutes. As the first generation to grow up entirely in the postmodern era, GenXers have been educated by a secularized public school system to believe that all truth is relative and personal. For them truth is relational rather than propositional. They will be attracted to experiencing a friendship with God more than knowledge about God.

• They do not trust institutions. The church, as an institution, holds little interest for them even though church in a relational sense may be very attractive.

• Their quest is for meaning and purpose, though they no longer have faith in traditional modes of religious expression or in the previous generation's fascination with "scientific objectivity." They will inevitably ask, "How does it affect me?"

• They are sometimes pessimistic. Those whose pilgrimages toward meaning and understanding are less than fulfilling often veer toward despair. "The suicide rate for teens has doubled since 1968, and the number of children using drugs by the sixth grade has tripled since 1975."[7]

• They are open to God, but not always to religion. It sounds arrogant to young adults to suggest that your truth is better than someone else's or that you have "the truth."

• They highly value authenticity and personal integrity. More impressive than a coherent philosophical system is the transparent life of a Christian who is genuine and open.

• They are not easy to categorize or understand. Postmodern young adults have an amazing capacity to live with paradoxes, both in their lives and in their world views. To contradictions that distress older generations, they often respond with a favorite expression, "Whatever."

Keeping young adults in the church. Growth in understanding and responding to the needs of young adults will characterize congregations that retain those who join their ranks from this target generation. Such churches seek ways to:

• Develop community. Churches have a marvelous opportunity to live out their faith through small groups where deep and lasting friendships with God and with each other are formed.

• Provide a sense of worship. Young adults want to lead their own groups, meetings, and projects. Giving them a sense of ownership means stepping aside and entrusting young adults with responsibilities based on their talents and interests.

• Be practical. Young adults prefer action to talk. They favor projects with local relevance where tangible results can be seen. Hands-on involvement in ministry such as serving meals in a homeless shelter, building and restoring homes for people in need, and mentoring children and teens through "big sibling" relationships allows them to translate faith into action.

• Be friendly. Beyond relationships with peers, young adults are looking for authentic, mutual relationships with older adults. Opportunities for development of intergenerational friendships can help keep young adults in the church.

• Help them find their niche. Rather than plugging young adults into predefined roles, churches that are serious about retaining their young adults will assess the gifts, temperaments, and spiritual passions of members and seek to involve them in challenging areas for which they feel most suited—e.g., video production, computer graphics, contemporary music, and arts. Again, more impressive than a coherent philosophical system are the transparent lives of Christians who are genuine and open.

• Continue to learn and grow. Form a focus group or advisory council of young adults to guide the church in discipling young members.

• Create new worship experiences where young adults encounter God. Services must be interactive, employ story and drama, and give young adults room both to search for and to form their own conclusions. Music must be joyous, creative, and in a familiar idiom. Excellence must be pursued throughout.

• Present a message of good news and hope. There has never been a generation more ready to hear and respond to

Christ's invitation to belong to Him, to experience authentic friendship with God, and to live in authentic fellowship in a community of faith than in today's young people.

Revealing God's character of love

This is where the action is! "The last rays of merciful light, the last message of mercy to be given to the world is a revelation of [God's] character of love."[8]

Pastor Nelson suggested two practical things pastors and churches can do.

"First, we have got to start building bridges with [people of all backgrounds] now. You cannot wait until opening night and drag them in and say, 'Here's Dwight.' You've got to go out and love people.

"Second, along with the loving, there must be an intensive praying. . . . Forward on our knees! That's the only way we can go."[9] We can keep them if we care!

---

[1] "NET '98 Getting Relational." An interview with Dwight Nelson by Andy Nash. *Adventist Review*, April 1998, 13.

[2] The host congregation was the Pioneer Memorial Seventh-day Adventist Church on the campus of Andrews University, Berrien Springs, Michigan.

[3] *Adventist Review*, April 1998, 12, 13.

[4] I am indebted to several young adult ministry specialists for insights presented in this column: Don Keele, Jr., is a creative youth and young adults pastor in Georgia; A. Allan Martin, a pastor and church consultant in California, and Andy Nash, an assistant editor of the *Adventist Review*, are both GenXers and write extensively about young adult ministries and issues; Ron Preast is a pastor, evangelist, and academy Bible teacher in Washington State and his wife, Jeanene, is an academy chaplain; my brother, John Cress, is chaplain of Walla Walla College, as well as the father of two GenXers.

[5] Quoted in Tim Celek and Dieter Zander, *Inside the Soul of a New Generation* (Grand Rapids: Zondervan, 1996), 22.

[6] Ibid., 36.

[7] Ibid., 50.

[8] Ellen G. White, *Christ's Object Lessons* (Hagerstown, Md.: Review and Herald Publishing Association, 1900), 415.

[9] *Adventist Review*, April 1998, 12, 13.

THE POWER OF
GOD'S WORD

Preaching the Word of God is life changing. Recently, I completed presenting a series of public meetings on the great themes of Scripture. About two dozen individuals responded by requesting baptism, which is a credit to the quality of the pastor and congregation with whom I worked as well as to the continuing power of God's Word to impact the lives of those who hear the good news.

Furthermore, I am personally refreshed anew by experienc-ing the impact that preaching the message had upon my own life—my ears heard the good news even from my own tongue, and my soul rejoices in God's graciousness.

Although the resulting numbers of new believers vary from situation to situation, invariably lives are changed when God's Word is proclaimed. I encourage you to renew your own experience and to witness the ongoing power of Scripture by actively proclaiming the following realities of the Word of God.

The Eternal Word. First, and foremost, the Word of God is a person, the individual Jesus Christ. When you preach the message of Scripture, your listeners encounter more than themes, theory, or theology. They encounter the One who was in the beginning, the Word that was with God, who remains eternal with God, who created all things, and who is very God, Himself (John 1:1-3). No wonder the prophet declares "the Word of God stands forever" (Isaiah 40:8).

The Incarnate Word. Glorious reminder of the gospel message–God with us! When seeking to save the lost, God did not look down from above and pull us up to heaven's expectations. Rather, Jesus emptied Himself and became human, taking upon Himself our very nature and our experience in order to lift us up with Himself into heavenly place (Philippians 2:5-11). To accomplish our salvation, "the Word was made flesh and dwelt among us" (John 1:14).

The revealed Word. Knowing that all people throughout history would not have personal access to the public ministry of Jesus when He was on earth, God also purposed to reveal His secrets to His servants, the prophets, in order to communicate His love, His purposes, and His grace to lost humanity (Amos 3:7). Using earthly humans to communicate heavenly concepts, God's Word reveals His saving intent. You extend that prophetic ministry today when you proclaim the good news of God's Word.

The written Word. To perpetuate the faithful witness of His messages, God's Holy Spirit brought light and surety even in dark places by the prophetic word. These messages did not come about by human invention, nor by the will of man. Rather, godly individuals spoke as they were moved by the Holy Spirit (2 Peter 1:19-21). Thus the recorded Word of God, the Scriptures, truly is God's words for our own lives and the lives of those to whom we minister.

The proclaimed Word. Power accompanies the preaching of God's Word. In fact, although it may seem foolish to depend upon personal proclamation in an age of multimedia communication options, the Scriptural promise remains true—faith comes by hearing and hearing by the Word of God (Romans 10:17). Something powerful occurs when any individual asks God's blessing upon our efforts to effectively communicate His message to the lost. Faith is awakened as the Word is opened.

The saving Word. God's Word comes with the specific purpose to save the lost—"having been born again, through the Word of God which lives and abides forever" (1 Peter 1:23).

By feeding upon Christ's body and His blood—the words which Christ spoke—we become partakers of the divine nature (2 Peter 1:4). Do you want to become more like Jesus? Spend more time feasting upon Him through His words.

The teaching Word. The power of the Holy Scriptures still makes people wise unto salvation through faith in Christ Jesus. A fourfold purpose of Scripture is to teach us sound doctrine about Jesus, to reprove our rebellious wanderings away from Jesus, to correct our steps back to Jesus, to instruct us in the continuing walk with Jesus, and to completely equip us for loving service in Jesus (2 Timothy 3:15-17). Even the very stories of Scripture are told with the purpose of teaching us about how to live within God's plan for our lives (Romans 15:4).

The authoritative Word. When Jesus personally spoke, He came with an authority beyond human capability or reasoning (Mark 1:22). Today, His Word remains authoritative for all people of all time. God clearly warns against adding to or detracting from God's Word by including our own pet theories or excluding His own clear instructions (Revelation 22:18,19).

In an age that resists authority, God's Word remains the rock upon which His people can securely fasten. "The reason many in this age of the world make no greater advancement in the divine life is because they interpret the will of God to be just what they will to do. While following their own desires, they flatter themselves that they are conforming to God's will."[1]

The transforming Word. Jesus will receive me, "just as I am." But through the transforming power of His Word, He will take me "just where He wants me to be." Our Lord prayed, "sanctify them through Thy truth, Thy Word is truth" (John 17:17). The Word of God has power to sanctify our lives as it effectively works in the lives of believers (1 Thessalonians 2:13). The Scriptures have such power that we can be kept from sinning by feeding deeply upon the Word (Psalm 119:9, 11).

"With the growing contempt for God's law, there is an increasing distaste for religion, an increase of pride, love of pleasure, disobedience to parents, and self-indulgence ... What can be done to correct these alarming evils? The answer is ... 'Preach the Word.' In the Bible are found the only safe principles of action. It is a transcript of the will of God, an expression of divine wisdom. It opens to man's understanding the great problems of life; and to all who heed its precepts, it will prove an unerring guide, keeping them from wasting their lives in misdirected effort."[2]

The Living Word. Finally, God anticipates that His Word will take root in the lives of His followers so that they, too, will become living epistles of His saving grace. As the little children sing, "Don't you know, O' Christian, you're a sermon in shoes." Our lives, known and observed by others may be the only sermon that some individuals will ever hear (2 Cor. 2:2, 3).

The influence of a godly life in an ungodly world has powerful impact for the saving of souls. Many who would never darken the door of a church to hear you or any other speaker preach the Scriptures, will have their hearts warmed by your living epistle that spreads the good news in the midst of your daily activities.

[1] Ellen G. White, *Acts of the Apostles* (Nampa, Idaho: Pacific Press Publishing Association, 1911), 565.

[2] Ibid., 506.

CONSERVING THE CATCH

Again, the kingdom of heaven is like a dragnet that was cast into the sea and gathered some of every kind, which, when it was full, they drew to shore; and they sat down and gathered the good into vessels, but threw the bad away. So it will be at the end of the age. The angels will come forth, [and] separate the wicked from among the just. — Matthew 13:47-49

Adventists doing the work of angels! Many times that is expressed in charitable, self-denying, and benevolent actions. But with regard to new believers, too often we do that which Jesus says must be reserved for the day of judgment and for angels who will serve as God's agents.

We want to sort the catch. We want to discard the bad. We want to stop fishing and start evaluating the catch. In short, we want to judge.

Jesus took the illustration from everyday life—a large net, pulled by boats, gathering all in its path. If it were possible for the dragnet to select only that which is edible, clean, and palatable, then the eventual process of sorting, preserving, and discarding would be unnecessary.

However, this is not the function of the dragnet. It gathers all that it sweeps across, and all remain together until the time the fisherman, not the fish, do the evaluation (judgment).

This parable is not a depiction of one-to-one, personal evangelism; it is far more inclusive. It is all-embracing in its scope. As Chaney and Lewis say: "Most modern evangelicals who, if they fish at all, fish for sport, have misunderstood the figure Jesus used. They think of a fisherman as a man who uses a rod, line, and lure. Fishing is a one-on-one proposition. In this way, this text has been used to encourage modern Christians to become personal evangelists. The early disciples fished with nets. Fish were in schools, hopefully, and were certainly not caught one at a time. Growing churches have captured that vision. They have learned how to fish with nets."[1]

This parable teaches two clear lessons. First, God expects great numbers to be gathered in. Second, He expects the church to cope with the reality that both good and bad will be caught.

The good and the bad

Like the parable of the wheat and tares (Matt. 13:24-30), the parable of the dragnet demonstrates that both good and bad will remain together until the end of the world. These two parables also avoid a separation that prevents the people of God from associating with the people of the world. We are to be in the world, but not of the world.

Unlike other theological models for developing disciples or nurturing newborns, this parable does not deal with any transition or process from bad to good or from good to bad, but simply asserts the fact that both exist together in the same environment. That environment is the church.

Jesus clearly teaches that it is the role of the church to nurture new believers more than to evaluate them. Peter Wagner says, "In the early stages of growth it is sometimes difficult to tell true disciples from counterfeits. But that judgment is not usually the responsibility of the evangelist who is concerned more with discipling then perfecting."[2] The church's role is to take that new believer into full discipleship where his character can enter the discipline of being perfected.

Jesus does not envision the church as a "holier than thou" club that stands over against the rest of the world. Just as He ate with publicans and sinners, so His disciples will move and live among people who do not believe, as well as among those who do believe, and yet who behave badly.

The dragnet allows for variety, and the possibility of undesirable fish being part of the catch. "Men are all alike sinners, but not sinners alike."[3]

Some of those sinners, and a good deal of their misbehavior, will be exhibited within the milieu of the congregation. Of course, much of this misbehavior will occur in the lives of new believers (those most recently pulled in by the dragnet).

If we understand the implications of nurturing newborns, this energetic misbehavior is to be expected. If we understand the imperative of discipling, then we know that the same misbehavior is to be carefully corrected and developed into appropriate behavior and fruitful discipleship. Both of these objectives are mandated.

But either way, discarding the bad from the catch is the work of angels. That's not our job!

[1] Charles L. Chaney and Ron S. Lewis, *Design for Church Growth* (Nashville: Broadman Press, 1977).

[2] C. Peter Wagner, *Church Growth and the Whole Gospel* (San Francisco: Harper and Row, 1981), p. 140.

[3] Myron S. Augsburger, *The Communicator's Commentary: Matthew* (Waco, Texas: Word Books, 1982), p. 179.

REAL LIFE
CHURCH PLANTING

Herb Larson, Jr., is an industrial design engineer, musical composer, arranger and performer, educational consultant, artist, and illustrator.

He is also a church planter.

I talked with this preacher's kid about the dream-to-reality process by which he and his wife, Tamara, along with four friends, planted the Open Door Seventh-day Adventist Church in Vancouver. Herb's enthusiasm for church planting is exceeded only by his joy in his personal relationship with Jesus.

But things were not always that way. Just six years ago Herb awakened one Sabbath to the reality that he did not want to go to church. Not then. Not ever! Most of his forty-something age friends had already abandoned church. Herb felt he was about to join them.

But not yet. As he prayed about his spiritual lethargy, Herb visioned a church he wished he could attend. Not knowing of any that fit the description, he determined to plant one.

Today as many as 200 people (about 50 more than the baptized membership) worship weekly. Here's what I learned from Herb about church planting:

Prepare thoroughly. Too many good projects fail because of unbridled enthusiasm. A project without a plan is a failure. For a full year, Herb led a group of six believers in weekly sessions of planning, praying, and visioning their new church. They checked out various worship styles, researched why members drop out, and projected what it would take to reclaim inactives.

Start fresh. This group quickly realized the futility of forcing existing congregations to change. They wanted the support of sister churches, but they hesitated to hamper revival with resistance from those who might insist that traditions were correct because "we've always done it that way!"

Earn support. Determined to stay close to denominational structure, they gained the backing of conference leaders and began a process of informing sister churches of their plans, hosting discussion sessions, and sharing their vision.

They determined not to change any traditional approach to church just for the sake of being different. In fact, they selected one of their group as the *"Church Manual* expert" to keep their church in line with established policies.

Provide quality. One common frustration expressed by former members was the "same old stuff." Herb's group covenanted that they would provide quality in every expression of worship. They regularly put 40 to 50 hours of planning into every worship service. A scheduled speaker is requested to submit a full sermon outline six weeks in advance. The message drives the theme of worship—in music, prayers, dialogues, skits, appeals, and testimonies.

Uplift Jesus. The Saviour is central. Herb and his group know the power of the name of Jesus. Their advance planning guarantees that every sermon builds a relationship with Jesus. They understand that the primary reason people drop out of church is lack of relationship with Jesus and involvement in the church.

Involve everyone. Attendees are immediately treated as members. In fact, associate membership status is officially recognized for those "regulars" who are "on the way." Anyone is welcome, and all are encouraged to participate. Typically over two dozen individuals are "up front" at every worship service.

Recruit by gifts. Although they now have a full-time pastor, Open Door intentionally began as a laity-led project. Church offices are structured to the need. They diligently avoid ladder climbing, power tripping, and striving for position. Decisions are more processed than voted. The conference recruited their pastor carefully to serve more as a facilitator than as a director. The members readily embrace both the privilege and the responsibility for making their church function.

Involve community. Beyond reclaiming former members, Open Door fully understands mission. The church hosts regular social, spiritual, and educational events for the public. A recent "Festival in the Park" attracted wide media attention and good attendance. Worship services are held in a high-quality public auditorium.

Evaluate progress. The members regularly evaluate every facet of the church—even the pastor's sermons. They consistently ask, "How can we do better?" Feedback is sought and shared.

Expand by example. Others can learn from their experience at quarterly seminars that teach all areas of what this congregation has learned as they have rediscovered joy in Jesus and His church!

CARING IN THE
AGE OF AIDS

My friend and colleague, Eldon E. Carman, who directed the Adventist dental mission program for many years, recently discussed his post-retirement ministry of counseling HIV-positive individuals.

Comparing HIV and its resulting AIDS pandemic to leprosy of biblical days, Carman shared his reasons for volunteering 20 hours per week counseling those who seek anonymous testing and who must then wait three weeks to determine whether they face a potential death sentence.

"While traveling the world to establish dental clinics, I observed the devastating results of HIV. After my wife's death, I wanted to serve others. If I can help one individual, practically and spiritually, then my efforts will be worthwhile." Carman's work includes specific insights and actions that help churches to minister more effectively in the age of AIDS.

AIDS is not just a homosexual disease. Although the AIDS epidemic in North America spread first and most rapidly among male homosexuals, today the HIV situation mirrors the rest of the world and affects heterosexuals more significantly than we imagine. By the year 2000, more women than men are expected to be infected with HIV. Few congregations and virtually no extended families will remain untouched by a member infected with HIV.

Knowledge of risk does not prevent the consequences of foolish behavior. Many individuals who come to clinics for HIV testing report that their contact was from a casual sexual encounter, often with their judgment impaired by

43

alcohol. Now they want to protect their spouse or potential partner from consequences they fear they have brought upon themselves. Grief and embarrassment at their own foolishness are typical expressions of many heterosexuals. Denial and hopeless fatalism are the reactions of many homosexuals.

Innocent people can be infected with HIV by their irresponsible partners. Today there is little chance of being infected from blood transfusions in North America because of an aggressive campaign to protect the blood supply. But children born to drug users are at great risk, as is anyone who shares an injection needle.

Regardless of how they became infected, individuals with HIV need kindness and empathy. Jesus reached out to those of His day who were infected with leprosy. His followers express His ministry by serving those who suffer from this plague. The church must talk about how to prevent HIV and how to minister to those infected.

Not everyone with HIV will develop AIDS, but every individual with AIDS has previously contracted the HIV virus. Adults would be amazed at the ignorance of young people about basic facts of anatomy, bodily functions, and sexuality. The church should help parents find ways to teach their youngsters how to live chaste, informed, and responsible lives in a world saturated with temptation and opportunities for immorality.

Love, acceptance, and forgiveness must be communicated. Jesus is just as willing to forgive the sin of judgmentalism as He is the sins of sexual promiscuity. If the church will do Christ's will, it must love the sinner though despising the sin. The church must provide a safe haven for those who have fallen victim to Satan's temptations and who desire a place to begin again. Followers of Jesus can be supportive of sinners without condoning their actions. We must communicate the inseparable principles of Jesus that sinners are welcome here as well as to go and sin no more! If the church fails to minister, who will communicate God's plan for restoration?

Christians have historically provided leadership in health care and education. No less today, the community needs to know that believers are interested in every disease that sin inflicts and that Jesus is the true Balm of Gilead to heal sin-sick souls. Your church could participate in a community health fair by distributing HIV prevention and drug prevention information.

Support groups offer opportunities to serve. Congregations can host recovery groups, education forums, blood drives, parenting classes, and other community services. Individual members can volunteer in schools, counseling centers, crisis lines, and hospices.

AIDS patients are often isolated and lonely. They need food preparation and delivery, assistance with errands, transportation, and, above all, simple friendship that communicates Jesus' love. None should wonder whether the church cares about the wider community. The community will readily refer seekers to a church that expresses caring nurture for those in trauma.

Support can be extended to the families of those affected by AIDS. Many are fearful of what has attacked their own reputation or standing in society as a result of a relative with HIV. Compassionate expressions of understanding friendship may help a frightened fellow member face the uncertain tomorrows for a family member they love. Offering a word of encouragement or sharing a prayer of support is real ministry.

Above all else, it is our privilege to offer hope. Hope for release from sin, hope for abundant life now, and hope for restoration and eternal life at Jesus' return.

Blessed hope! Blessed assurance! When the church communicates this hope, it is Christ's body at its best!

MAKING YOUR SCHOOL
SUCCESSFUL

Your church school's success depends on your personal support. Leaders have both the privilege and the responsibility to promote Christian education. Now is the time to help make your school's next term even better. To give less than your best effort to Christian education is to fail one of our greatest mission opportunities: our own children.

Beyond advocating that parents should place their children in Christian schools, you can take the following positive actions to assure that the schools under your watchcare will thrive.

Plan for growth. Never be satisfied with the status quo if there is one child who could be enrolled. With only about half of Adventist children attending our parochial schools, opportunities abound. Challenge your church and school boards to develop school-growth eyes. Vision for growth expands only to the extent that leaders set the pace. So think growth yourself and encourage others to see the mission potential of a growing school.

Affirm Christian education both by word and action. Preach the value of Christian schools versus public education and maintain the emphasis of reaching and holding our own young people. You may wish to invite the conference education director to speak to your congregation.

Match your rhetoric with action. If you have children, enroll them in church school. If personal circumstances prevent you from enrolling your children in your church's school, request assignment to a district that does not have a school. Your example, as well as your words, must signal clear support for Christian education.

Affirm the ministry of teaching. Honor your teachers in front of the whole congregation for the sacrificial ministry they provide. Seek ways to express appreciation for your teachers and to acknowledge their successes. Support school activities by your attendance at functions they plan.

Acknowledge the contribution of your school in public ways such as a dedication service at the start of each school year in which you offer special prayer for teachers and students, or a special Sabbath service in which the school plans and leads the worship service. Try a Teacher Recognition Sabbath in which you present a gift to each of the teachers and tell of his personal ministry to the church. Also, credit your teachers' influence on the spiritual decisions that children make.

Encourage parents to prioritize. Help them understand that Adventist schools are not only different from public education, but also are distinctly different from other Christian schools. Adventist atmosphere, lifestyle, and doctrine pervade all curriculum subjects. If parents want their children to grow up in the church, they should enroll them in the church school.

Help teachers. Assist in planning programs that will exhibit the value of your school such as open houses or school visitation days. Conduct chapel services and special weeks of Spiritual Emphasis for the students. Offer to teach a class once or twice per year or to serve occasionally as a substitute teacher. Drive for a field trip, or just stop by the school to chat with students and teachers during recess or lunch breaks. Welcome the students on the first day of the term.

Make recruiting visits. Go with your teachers to the homes of all potential students. Nothing makes a greater impact than the pastor and teacher together visiting the home of each family with school-age children. These visits should include an invitation to place the children in your school, along with helpful information about registration processes, a school calendar, financial plans that are available, and preferably some memento of your visit for each potential student. By the way, don't take returning students for granted. They also deserve a visit.

Furthermore, those families who already recognize the benefit of church school can be one of your best sources for locating other potential students. Ask each family you visit if they know of someone else who could be invited to enroll in your school.

Encourage experimentation. For families who wonder if Adventist schools are really best, offer a money-back guarantee. In my own pastorate, we encouraged parents to enroll their children experimentally, with the guarantee of fees and tuition refunded if they were dissatisfied and enrolled their children elsewhere. The school rarely had anyone ask for a refund. The parents' experiment demonstrated the worth of our school.

Raise assistance funds. Not every family can pay full tuition and fees. Their children also need to be in your school. I enjoy helping my members realize that we operate a "church" school and not just a "parent" school, and I enjoy raising money to assist worthy students who otherwise would be unable to attend. Every parent should contribute something, but never prevent anyone from attending because of lack of funds.

Develop a work-study program. Older students can make a helpful contribution to the school or church by performing tasks that otherwise would be hired out. The funds you would have spent to have someone empty the trash, answer the telephone, wash windows, sweep sidewalks, fold and insert letters and bulletins, or vacuum floors might easily be accomplished by a student in a few hours after school.

Remember the mission. Adventist schools should be

evangelistic. I have seen whole families baptized whose first contact with the church was enrolling their children in the school. If you have available space, recruit nonmember students whose families will be a great source of potential new members.

After all, Adventist education is a mission!

THE FINE ART OF
PASTORAL VISITATION

S ome believe pastoral visitation is dead. However, when members describe qualities of the ideal pastor, they typically list visitation as a high priority.

While societal trends may change expectations, most members still welcome a personal visit from their pastor. When I surveyed my urban members on their desire for visitation, most indicated their strong preference for visitation only by appointment. Other pastors say that their members have different expectations and want the pastor to "drop in" anytime.

Pastoral visitation is not dead. It may be bungled at best or ignored at worst, but it remains a fine art that brings enormous benefits when rightly practiced. Consider the following suggestions:

View visitation as spiritual work in which you minister to your members and extend Christ's kingdom by inviting others to accept His Lordship. "There are families who will never be reached by the truth of God's Word unless His servants enter their homes, and by earnest ministry, sanctified by the endorsement of the Holy Spirit, break down the barriers. As the people see that these workers are messengers of mercy, the ministers of grace, they are ready to listen to the words spoken by them."[1]

Announce your intentions. Let your members know the conditions under which you will visit. For example, I informed my members that I would visit either by their invitation or by my initiation, but I would not visit without an appointment. I also shared with them that they would receive a pastoral visit when they were hospitalized, but that such a visit might be provided by one of the local church elders who also serve as part of the pastoral-care team.

Make visitation a priority. Set aside a specific time each week for visitation. If you fail to prioritize specific visitation time, other demands will prevent you from acting on your good intentions. Contact visitors to your church immediately after their attendance. You should also visit members who may be experiencing challenges or crisis situations, those who have initiated contact with radio or television programs, others who are potential members, and, especially, your nonattending members.

Do not visit alone. Taking an elder with you has its advantages. It's in accordance with Christ's example of sending out His disciples two by two. It is also a good technique for self-preservation. Why risk damaging your reputation because of what others might report you said or did when you were in their home alone? It helps train your laity. If a person whom you visit needs to begin Bible studies, you can immediately turn that contact over to the elder who has accompanied you.

Mentor by association. You will enlarge the vision of your laity leaders by taking them with you. They will see that this work of visitation is important to you, and they will come to believe that they could reproduce your skills because they have observed you doing it rather than telling about it.

Conserve your time. Ask some individuals to come to you rather than you traveling to them. Set up appointments for Bible studies or counseling sessions at your church for those who can easily commute there. Bunching your visits in a specific section of the city or an area of your district also helps.

Make short visits. A visit need not be everlasting in order to have eternal benefit. In the hospital, tell your parishioner that you have stopped by to pray for his need. Encourage him that God cares. Ask if he have a prayer request. Share a Scripture promise and pray for his need. Meet other patients in the same room and include them in prayer.

In evangelistic visits you can usually accomplish more in five or ten minutes than if you stay an hour. Clearly state the purpose of your visit by giving the individual a tract or booklet about a topic you have recently preached. Thank him for attending your meetings. Ask an open-ended question regarding his receptiveness to what he is hearing, and request permission to pray a blessing upon the home before you leave. Your brevity and spiritual emphasis will signal the importance of the issues about which you are preaching.

[1] Ellen G. White, *Evangelism* (Washington, D.C.; Review and Herald Publishing Association, 1946), pp. 435, 436.

EVERY SERMON
SHOULD
CALL FOR A RESPONSE

Why did you preach last Sabbath's sermon? Did you expect your listeners to do something in response? Or were you just filling the time between offering and benediction?

Perhaps it's time we rethink preaching. Perhaps the times demand that we think about intentional preaching—preaching on purpose! Intentional preaching involves planning what you will say and what you expect in response from your audience.

A sermon that does not demand a response is not a sermon. It may be a discussion, a presentation, a monologue, or even cleverly disguised religious entertainment, but not a sermon. Unless what you preach motivates the audience toward some positive reaction to what they have heard, your sermon is incomplete.

Peter's sermon at Pentecost was so powerful that the listeners made the appeal themselves: "Now when they heard this, they were pricked in their heart, and said unto Peter and to the rest of the apostles, 'Men and brethren, what shall we do?'" (Acts 2:37). Unless you can preach with such power and conviction, it will be necessary for you to make your own appeal to extend an invitation that calls for a response.

In fact, planning your appeal before you construct your sermon is one of the greatest tools in building a powerful sermon. Ask yourself, "What action do I want my audience to take as a result of this message?" The question will change not only your sermon but also your sermon preparation. The process will be different because your objective will be clearly delineated at the beginning. Everything you say will be focused toward the goal of motivating the desired response.

When I first told my congregation that I would extend an appeal at the close of every sermon, they reacted with surprise. But soon they discovered that the appeal not only guided my sermon preparation each week, but also demanded a balanced schedule of texts and topics throughout the year.

Further, an invitation every week requires careful worship planning in order to allow sufficient time to accomplish the spiritual business at the end of every sermon.

How can you implement an appeal into your weekly worship service?

Condition your audience to expect an appeal after every sermon. Also, tell them your intention at the beginning of the sermon: *I intend to give you an opportunity to respond to Jesus Christ today.* If your audience knows that a response is expected from them, they will listen to the sermon differently and permit the Holy Spirit to work more effectively.

Prepare your audience for an appeal by preaching a Christ-centered sermon. "The object of preaching is not alone to convey information, not merely to convince the intellect. The preaching of the word should appeal to the intellect, and should impart knowledge, but it should do more than this. The words of the minister should reach the hearts of the hearers."[1] Sermons rooted in Jesus and bathed in the good news of salvation through the power of the Holy Spirit will reach the hearts of your hearers!

Establish a familiar routine for your appeals. This assures your congregation that the appeal is planned as a vital part of your worship service and allows a person to think ahead to decisions that need to be made.

For ongoing use, a generic response card is quite helpful. Such a card could include opportunities to accept Jesus as personal Saviour, to request baptism or church membership (by profession of faith), to request prayer about specific needs, as well as requests for Bible studies, pastoral visits, etc.

Because I wanted my members to respond every week (attendance records), I found it helpful to include some choices to which they could always respond: *I would like the Holy Spirit to continue working in my life; pray that I will personally apply the lesson of* _____ *from today's sermon.*

Allow sufficient time. In order to allow ample opportunity for my hearers to respond, I arrange a musical presentation each week at the time of the appeal. The musical selection for the appeal should clearly focus on the heart, and, typically, the presentation should be vocal rather than instrumental. It is preferable to have a familiar singer from the congregation rather than a visiting musician who might attract the audience to his uniqueness rather than to the decision-making process.

Consider each response an opportunity to minister. My members appreciated a postcard or telephone call assuring them that I had seen their requests for special prayer and would, indeed, remember them that week. Guests always received acknowledgment of their responses. Even if they only registered their attendance, they received a note expressing appreciation for their visit. Always prioritize those who are seeking further Bible studies, acceptance of Jesus Christ, or baptism. During one year we had more than 50 requests for baptism.

Begin now. Ask the Holy Spirit to make you willing to extend regular appeals and to give you fruit for your labor.

[1] Ellen G. White, *Testimonies to Ministers* (Mountain View, Calif.: Pacific Press Publishing Association, 1923), p. 62.

COMMON SENSE
PASTORING

What do pastors most need to accomplish their ministry? After personal spirituality—a daily walk with Jesus Christ—I would suggest the next essential is common sense.

The very term "common sense" is an oxymoron since its possession is an uncommon trait. Likewise, the term is difficult to define because like water held in our hands, common sense is more difficult to grasp than it is to observe.

Common sense may best be described by the Greek word *phronesis,* meaning "practical wisdom," which Aristotle considered to be about the most important of all virtues.

Common sense pastoring suggests that practical wisdom reigns over theoretical concepts. It suggests that head knowledge is most effective when applied to useful experience in the crucible of daily life.

Common sense means thoroughly examining any idea for its real-life usefulness. In other words, the genius of common sense is application more than description. To use the vernacular of the automobile tire moving the vehicle, common sense is "where the rubber meets the road."

Those who lack common sense usually outnumber those who possess it to such an extent that the few who actually utilize common sense are considered gifted. I disagree.

While pastors sometimes bring about their own defeat by failing to employ common sense, I believe that it is a skill that can be learned and sharpened.

I reject the popular concept that either you are born with common sense or you will never possess it at all. While many individuals innately focus on practical applications more readily than some of their peers, I am convinced that certain methods can be used to gain a practical quality of wisdom, if an individual is willing to pay the price for this knowledge. What would it cost you personally to embrace the following concepts?

Attitude is more important than aptitude. Placing yourself in the position of a seeker is vastly more important than considering yourself to be the fountain of knowledge. If you believe that you have all the answers, you will seldom ask the important questions. If you believe your opinion is more valuable than all others, you will seldom listen to the wisdom that begs for entrance to your closed mind. If your way is the only way of doing things, you need an attitude adjustment.

What you learned yesterday is more important that what you do today. Experience is a difficult teacher. She gives the test first and the lesson afterward. Common sense can be learned from what worked or failed in your own past experience. Capitalize on that knowledge now. Grow from the challenges you have already faced.

Trying something different may be the wisest course. Repetition for the sake of consistency destroys progress. Recently I read this definition of insanity: "doing the same things over and over and expecting different results." If change is needed, set a vision for the future and invite your members to move forward with you.

Trying something different may be the most risky course. Any change costs something. Some members will resist any innovation, so alterations just for the sake of change may be foolish. Carefully learn the history of your church. Your congregation has a story that has brought it to today's situation. Build on your church's strengths and apply what you have learned from the past. Make sure that your leaders are with you and willing to help pay the cost.

Offer alternatives rather than making all the decisions yourself. Common sense pastoring means seeking consensus in any matter that does not involve moral issues. Pastors should also remember that moral issues are far less in number than we might imagine. You are safe to confine such issues to the ten commandments. Matters such as the color of carpet, what songs are sung in Kindergarten, or who leads VBS crafts are seldom of such magnitude that they should ignite divisive controversy. Suggest alternatives to a committee for their selection or input. Then be willing to live with their choices.

Attempting something is more important than doing it perfectly. I am always amazed at how the Holy Spirit uses an atmosphere of evangelism in the congregation to reduce other problems. If you wait until you possess the expertise of a great evangelist, you may never get around to active outreach. However, if you use your talents to proclaim the gospel in a public presentation, you will discover heaven's blessings on both your efforts and your whole congregation.

So give it a try. Implement some practical activities right now. Reject the concept that yours is the only appropriate method. Try something new and breathe life into some of your traditional methods.

Common sense pastoring is an ongoing adventure which promises greater success tomorrow from what you put to use today.

TEN WAYS TO THANK
YOUR PASTOR

Because of the unique organizational structure of the Adventist Church, in which pastors are assigned by the conference committee and paid directly from the conference treasury, it is easy to forget that our local congregations have a significant role in the job satisfaction of their pastors.

Accepting God's call to ministry means accepting the high stress that accompanies any helping profession. You can personally increase your pastor's ministry motivation by supporting his or her ministry and expressing your appreciation. Below are ten ways you can support and encourage your pastor.

1. Volunteer. Most congregations have more work to be done than there are workers to accomplish the tasks. Some pastors try to do everything themselves and then burn out. Others see the enormity of the task and wish they could give up.

If you volunteer to do something, try to select a specific job you are willing to perform and then persist in volunteering until you are put to work.

2. Share in ministry. Offer to go with your pastor! Jesus sent His own disciples out two-by-two so they could encourage one another. You could lift your pastor's load by joining with him in pastoral visitation, giving Bible studies, conducting Revelation seminars and evangelistic meetings, or even in the myriad of minutia that must be accomplished. The work load is lighter when two people share the burden to see it done.

3. Provide for a pastoral resource fund. Most pastors are severely limited in the books, visual aids, and study resources they can afford to purchase. Growing numbers of congregations give a monthly amount (you might aim for 25 cents a month per member) into a pastoral resource fund, which is then used by the pastor to purchase self-development and study materials that directly improve pastoral ministry to the congregation through better preaching and increased satisfaction.

4. Minister to the pastor's family. Pastoral families are often deprived of time with their pastor-spouse or parent because the pastor's time is being given to the members. Why not insist that your pastor take an evening with his or her spouse while you baby-sit and fix dinner for their children?

Get together with several other members and sponsor your pastor to a continuing education seminar, and make it a special bonus by sending the spouse along. "Anyone who receives instruction in the word must share all good things with his instructor" (Galatians 6:6, NIV).

5. Celebrate pastoral anniversaries. Rather than decrying the short pastoral tenure of most Adventist ministers, celebrate the annual anniversary of your pastor's arrival in your church with a special worship service or a fellowship dinner celebration.

I know one congregation which gives a gift certificate to the pastor on each pastoral anniversary, while another plans a getaway vacation of one day per year of service to a nearby resort area. Our own congregation hosted a day-long Sabbath commemoration of our pastor's first anniversary in our midst.

Any pastor would be very reluctant to transfer from a congregation whose members express their appreciation. Affirmed pastors know the grass is greener right where they live!

6. Become a positive force in your congregation. Don't wait around for the pastor to come up with all the ideas. You will express appreciation to your pastor if you initiate some positive ideas and projects.

How about offering to coordinate a seminar for your church that will enable you and your fellow members to become better disciples as well as beginning to be disciple-makers. You might lead the plan for a new ministry for your community or organize a special event to draw guests to your church facilities.

7. Respect pastors. Most pastors are far busier than their members imagine. Moreover, pastors are on 24-hour call in one of the most highly-stressed environments possible. At the same time that their schedule is overloaded, they need creative time for study, reflection, and sermon preparation.

Always avoid denigrating comments such as "I wish I had the pastor's job—working only one day a week." Pastors will not always be perfect and may sometimes overlook a detail, but respect how much they do accomplish with the limited resources available.

8. Become a pastoral advocate. Speak up for your pastor to other members and, if you have an opportunity, affirm your pastor to conference leadership. Express written appreciation to conference administration for the pastoral care you receive and send your pastor a copy.

9. Verbally express your appreciation. Words cost nothing but mean so very much! A card or note of appreciation could make the gloomiest day seem bright.

Acknowledging an extraordinary sermon or a meaningful pastoral service will encourage your pastor to ongoing excellence. Make it your goal to express three affirmations for every complaint that comes to mind. You can be a modern Aaron or Hur, holding up the leader's hands.

10. Pray for your pastor and family. Much less faultfinding would occur if members were consistently praying for their pastors. If you have a problem with your pastor, that is the essential time to pray. And remember, when I pray for someone, it is not in order to change God's attitude toward that individual, but rather God changes my attitude toward the one for whom I am praying.

As well as praying for your pastor, also pray *with* your pastor. What an encouragement for pastors to actually hear a member praying aloud for them by name!

Nothing brings greater reward than providing encouragement and opportunities for pastors and their families which enhance their happiness in ministry and increase their effectiveness. Your entire church family will experience the positive consequences.

Stop right now and find a way to thank your pastor.

ANONYMOUS
ANIMOSITY

How do you handle hate mail when the senders are too cowardly to identify themselves?

Recently three people filled their pens with poison and targeted me. Praise God! At least when they were attacking me they were not after you.

Although aimed at me, these letters actually landed in my trash can. That's the final resting place of all unidentified mail that comes my way.

Normally anonymous letters don't arrive in my office three at a time. But whatever their frequency, I learned long ago to disregard them and even avoid reading them.

Thoughtful Christians may disagree strongly on a point and still respect each other, but I never respect someone who expects me to invest my time pondering their misguided missile without the courtesy of allowing me the opportunity to respond.

Here are a few suggestions for the occasions when you receive unsigned, unsolicited letters:

Remember that your supporters may fail to speak out. Many who appreciate your ministry overlook the importance of affirming you, since we usually express frustration more quickly than satisfaction.

Unsigned letters typically tear down rather than build up. Of course criticism has its proper place, and every leader needs honest input concerning shortcomings. However, appropriate criticism is constructive, meaning to construct, to build. Its aim is to improve the situation, not to blame or shame.

Resist taking anonymous criticism personally. Even though the attack upon you may be vicious, remember that conviction without courage is cowardice of the highest order. Refuse to become its victim.

Anonymous writers often lack full information. Armed with ignorance and undeserved fury, they fire at the nearest, most visible target—too often, the pastor. If they had full understanding of the issue, they might be supportive or, at least, remain neutral.

Rejoice if you are the target rather than someone else. I remember an unkind note slipped under my office door one Sabbath. The unsigned author ranted that the young people should have stayed away from church rather than to perform the music they had sung that morning. Although their music was not of my preference, I rejoiced that they were participating in worship. Had that anonymous hate-filled letter reached the youth, it might have discouraged them to the point of abandoning their music ministry and perhaps the church itself. I rejoice that it came to me instead.

Develop a distanced perspective. If you permit vicious criticism to sink in, it will gnaw at your psyche and destroy your self-confidence. This is precisely what your attacker wants. So let such messages roll off your back rather than sink into your soul. Another coping technique is to remember that members need to vent their frustrations from time to time and that you provide a real pastoral service when you are their focus for "recreational griping." This perspective also helps you shrug off bitterness that could easily germinate and take root in your soul.

Refuse to be paralyzed by the pessimists. Never permit an invisible minority, hiding behind code words such as "everyone agrees," "they all say," or "many believe," to destroy a good plan. I remember one visioning session in which an elder dreamed of tripling the size of our school enrollment.

Immediately, someone retorted, "But our building could not contain that many students." Another elder responded, "Never let today's reality stomp on tomorrow's dream." Now that same school has tripled its enrollment and doubled its facilities.

Become more proactive than reactive. If you pander to the naysayers, little effective ministry will occur. Instead, keep close counsel with your elders and other church leaders and then move ahead to accomplish God's vision for your church without stopping to worry about those who are forever chasing after you to bark at your wheels.

Model appropriate confrontation. If you want to reduce hidden messages or veiled threats, it helps to be open and above board in your own dealings. Do not conclude that problems will disappear if you let them go unchallenged. Follow Christ's counsel in Matthew 18 and speak directly to those with whom you disagree.

Seek appropriate anonymous input. Sometimes anonymous input is desirable. When surveying the opinion of the entire congregation or seeking input regarding the "buy in" of your members for a project or program, soliciting anonymous input by survey is healthy and informative.

Dispel rumors with humor. Several years ago false accusations abounded which alleged that many pastors were using hypnosis to control congregations. I answered with humor. Pointing to the financial statement, I remarked to my members, "Here is positive proof that you're not getting hypnotized. If you were, you would be giving lots more money!" The humor dispelled the rumor more effectively than any complex explanation or hot retort to an unfounded accusation.

Real friends will confront when something needs correction. In fact, such confrontation—*carefronting*—is an expression of love. "Faithful are the wounds of a friend; but the kisses of an enemy are deceitful" (Proverbs 27:6).

HELPING PKS ENJOY
PARSONAGE LIFE

A "preacher's kid" myself, I always thought I knew just how PKs ought to be raised. However, since I am not a parent, I have seldom acted on my inclination to advise pastoral parents on child-raising techniques.

In recent years, however, I have been increasingly concerned that fewer PKs follow their parents' example by choosing to enter ministry. Growing up in the parsonage gives young pastors an experiential advantage, and I wish that more PKs were hearing and accepting the call to ministry.

Virginia Smith, General Conference Children's Ministries Director, recently shared seven principles of helping PKs enjoy the parsonage. Parent of two PKs who, as adults, are directly involved in Christ's mission, Virginia speaks from both expertise and experience which are evident in the following points.

1. Become friends with your children. This is especially important for fathers. The way is the same as with any other friend. Invest time in being together with them. Build memories of the good times you enjoy together. Learn to know your children as individuals and to respect their individuality.

Your children are not your possession. They belong to God, and He has a plan for their lives. As you build a close relationship, you will bond them to you, and you will bond them to love the things you love—your work, your priorities, your objectives.

Studies demonstrate that fathers who spend adequate time with their daughters build a protective hedge against premarital sex because the young girls experience an appropriate male relationship at home. Similar evidence has been demonstrated for protection against drug abuse and other destructive behaviors.

2. Be supportive of expectations for ministers. It is essential for pastoral spouses to affirm the varied expectations for pastors. Your children will reflect your own attitudes toward the challenges that necessarily affect pastoral families. When interruptions come to your family, strive to uphold the importance of pastoral work to those who will benefit.

When your pastor spouse must travel, plan fun activities with your children. If both parents must travel, make the temporary care arrangements a special treat. Organize good supervision while you are away provided by someone who can relate well to your children's emotional needs. Then plan a special activity to celebrate your return when the family is reunited. Share what happened while you were separated and help your children understand the importance of your journey.

Listen carefully to their reports of what occurred in your absence. The most important information may well be disclosed only after they have talked with you for quite a while and may come out slowly, so take time to process their experiences. If your child's behavior has changed during your absence, likely something bad has happened. Become such good friends that your children feel comfortable telling you about their experiences.

3. Set high standards and help your children reach them. If you fill your kids' lives with Bible study, music, art, nature study, and athletics, there will be little time for television and computer games or to envy more affluent friends. Your home will become the center of happiness and the most attractive place for your children.

Likewise, make sure you are the provider of sex education for your children. Start early and naturally respond to their curiosity with information appropriate for their age and awareness. Do not assume that you should wait until they are older. If you wait, their first exposure to sexuality will likely be inaccurate and impure.

4. Involve your child in service for others. Help them to choose tasks they enjoy and to find a mission objective in their activities. Encourage them to participate with you in church activities. As you share ministry assignments together, their confidence will grow. Research shows that children learn more and faster when they actively participate. Thus they will become involved in church life by their own choice rather than becoming bored with religion. Provide age-appropriate activities that will help your PKs listen and participate during church services. Your goal is to help them choose, at their own initiative, to become involved in the Lord's work.

5. Invite your child to accept Christ. Don't assume they will "discover" a relationship with Jesus on their own. Provide regular religious nurture through family worship and periodically talk with them about their growing friendship with Jesus.

6. Protect your child from the church. Stand between them and members who criticize and expect too much from PKs. Let your children know that you want good behavior, but that you do not abandon them when they misbehave. Discuss incidents with your children and sympathize with their pain or frustration.

7. Give your children unconditional love. Relate to them as Jesus relates to all of us. After your children have passed the age when you can control their activities, they may make choices you dislike. At that time you have only two responsibilities: pray for them and remain their friends.

Once they are adults, do not expect to control their choices, their careers, or their homes. Your opportunity to influence their future is right now. Their first formative years provide you the opportunity to impact their lives for eternity.

WHEN YOUR REPUTATION
IS HELD HOSTAGE

Have you ever been held hostage by slander, surmisings, suspicions, misunderstandings, or circumstances beyond your control?

Whether it is the extreme ordeal of an untrue accusation of murder, as was faced by an Australian pastoral couple in the eighties, or linkage in the public view with the mindless actions of cultic or fringe groups, or even unjust conclusions and judgments about your motives by parishioners or church administrators, the impact is the same. Your good name, your reputation, is held hostage to what "they believe."

How should you react, especially when you know that you are innocent of the charges and that the actions that have been judged so wrong by others came from good intentions and benevolent motives?

Here are some suggestions that should help you develop an appropriate response.

Recognize your enemy. Our ultimate enemy, of course, is Satan, who delights in falsehood and misunderstanding and whose purpose is to obscure and hide the truth at every opportunity.

Often the immediate enemy appears in visible and tangible forms, promoting misunderstanding. Typically, however, the real enemy is not a person. Your enemy is much more likely the lack of opportunity to explain fully the facts, to analyze adequately all possible options, or to show how the misunderstood situation came to be fixed in other's minds.

Some people take time to listen and keep an open mind. Others reject even direct evidence that would correct their previously determined conclusions. What is your challenge? Is it to find time and place to review all the available information? Or is it preconceptions and closed minds?

Recognize your allies. Obviously, our heavenly Father is the greatest ally of all that is truthful and enlightening. Ask the Holy Spirit's help to speak appropriately the truth in love and to keep your hearers' hearts open to receive that which is accurate and factual.

If you choose to speak, a carefully reasoned recital of facts is preferable to an emotionally charged litany. When dealing with people problems, take extra steps to clarify situations and offer more than the minimum required opportunities for resolving conflict. Pay scrupulous attention to facts. Be prepared to document them. Avoid opinions and assumptions.

Just as the pressure of time can be an enemy to accuracy, so the passing of time can become a great ally. The old expression "time will tell" often proves to be the best solution. As events progress and evidence evolves, truth often becomes clear simply from falsehood's inability to sustain itself in the extended light of history.

Remember your options. Even in the midst of a challenging situation remember you do have options. You always have the choice to do nothing. Jesus often refused to answer His accusers. Likewise, you have the choice of saying nothing. Once uttered, words cannot be retrieved. Remember, no one can force you to discuss a topic on which you choose to remain silent.

Avoid judgmental categorization. Clearly state who you are, but carefully avoid characterizing others. Do not become an information resource or commentator on the actions, motives, beliefs, or thinking of individuals who differ with you or whose behavior may be holding your reputation hostage. Define yourself and your position and let others answer for their own actions or beliefs. Remember that when you "sling mud," you are always losing ground!

Take a long view. Look at things from the perspective of eternity and remember the promise that in all things—even bad things—God works for good for those who love Him and who are called according to His purpose (Romans 8:28).

In the midst of a crisis, you may reassess your own situation and determine that you must side with truth rather than leave error unchallenged. You may make eternal decisions prompted by the injustice of false accusations against the innocent.

In any event, remember that "this too shall pass." You can keep hope alive by focusing on that glad day when Jesus will return. Even so, come quickly, Lord Jesus!

JESUS, THE ESSENCE OF LIFE

In pastoral and evangelistic work, I am often requested to provide a brief summary of Adventist beliefs. A book, even one as excellent as the Ministerial Association's own *27 Fundamentals: Seventh-day Adventists Believe*, is too ponderous for such occasions.

I have also observed various "back of the bulletin" doctrinal summaries and thought too many of them provide only a proof-text database of information that misses the dynamic relational aspect of our life in Jesus.

Then I discovered an excellent little card at Hinsdale Hospital titled *Jesus, the Essence of Life.* I appreciated its Christocentric focus and freely adapted it for my own use. While this summary is not intended to replace the official statement of fundamental beliefs, it does provide an overview of our faith centered in the bedrock of a relationship with our Saviour. I printed it on a little card to share with those whose sincere queries deserve a Jesus-centered answer.

Jesus' Word is the Holy Scriptures. It was given by God to the prophets through an act of divine revelation and inspiration. The infallible revelation of Jesus' loving will for humanity is recorded in both the Old and New Testaments and contains all the knowledge necessary for salvation.

Jesus' Incarnation was God becoming fully human. Jesus the Son, the Father, and the Holy Spirit are a unity of three coeternal persons. Jesus, born of a virgin, is both our Creator and our Redeemer.

Jesus' voluntary death on the cross was a substitutionary sacrifice for our sins. According to the gospel (the good news!), when we accept by faith His perfectly obedient life and His substitutionary death, we are accounted as righteous before the Lord apart from any of our works. Jesus paid it all!

Jesus' resurrection is evidence that He has conquered the power of Satan and the power of death. It is the assurance given to His people of being resurrected at His coming and of living with Him throughout eternity. At the resurrection our mortal nature will receive from God immortality or eternal life.

Jesus' mediation in the heavenly sanctuary is an intercession on behalf of the human race. Enthroned at the right hand of the Father, His work as mediator now is also one of judgment, vindicating God's righteousness and vindicating His name and His people before the universe.

Jesus' character is a revelation of God's loving nature. The perception of His character has been distorted by Satan, resulting in a controversy that has brought into existence sin and untold suffering. One purpose of the plan of salvation is to unmask the deceiver and restore true recognition of Christ's immeasurable love and compassion.

Jesus' life is manifested today in His people through the agency of the Holy Spirit. He is Christ's representative on earth, the agent of the new birth, and the One who enables God's people to live victoriously. Through His power they order their Christian behavior on the basis of biblical principles and become stewards of God. Jesus bestows on His church spiritual gifts, including the gift of prophecy.

Jesus' obedience to the law of God revealed a perfect life free from sin. This righteous life which He offers is ours by faith. His obedience provides an example to His followers to keep God's commandments out of gratitude and love for what God has done for them.

Jesus' mission is performed today by His people as they proclaim the eternal gospel to the people of every nation and invite them to worship the Creator and call them to ultimate loyalty to the Lord.

Jesus' day occurs on the seventh day (Saturday) of each week. Jesus calls Himself Lord of this day and faithfully observed it. Instituted at Creation, the Sabbath is an appropriate memorial of God's creative power, but also a day of delightful communion with Him and one another. Formalized in the Ten Commandments, it is a symbol of our redemption in Christ, a sign of our sanctification, a token of our allegiance, and a foretaste of our eternal rest in God's kingdom.

Jesus' church is composed of all who confess Jesus Christ as Saviour and Lord. Believers come together for worship, for fellowship, for instruction in the Word, for the Lord's Supper, and for the proclamation of the gospel. Entrance into the church is through baptism by immersion as a visible expression of the new birth. In the last days God has selected from within the Christian community a remnant who keep the commandments of God and the faith of Jesus, and who call all people to prepare for the Second Coming of the Lord.

Jesus' return is assured. The prophetic proclamation of Scripture indicates that we are living in the last days and that His coming is rapidly approaching. This coming is personal, literal, physical, and visible. It will initiate a series of events that culminates in the destruction of evil forces, including Satan himself, the renewal of this planet, and the establishment of Christ's eternal kingdom of peace.

Jesus' invitation is for you. He wants to be your Saviour and the center of your life. He will enable you to live life abundantly now and to have the assurance of eternal life with Him in His soon-coming kingdom.

HOW TO DESTROY
YOUR LEADERSHIP

What destroys leadership? A boring committee meeting became a gold mine when a group of leaders turned from the routine to focus on issues that destroy leadership. Their points were enhanced by practical remedies.[1]

Issue: **Lack of credibility.** When leaders act differently than their expressed values, people lose confidence. If my life does not match my proclamation, people ultimately disbelieve my words.

Remedy: Beyond the obvious need for a closer walk with our Lord, which is integral to the remedy for all these areas, adherence to a code of ethics is essential. Situational leadership must never mean situational ethics.

Issue: **Incompetence.** Too often leaders reach a plateau of competence beyond which they no longer struggle to achieve. Settling for mediocre too often means abandoning excellence. Ideals and performance that once aimed high now rest in job security and accumulated years of service credit.

Remedy: Develop an atmosphere of growth. Break out of the routine, resist the humdrum. Stretch to establish and to reach your vision for the future. Head there. Others will follow!

Issue: **Self-service.** Leaders too easily develop an attitude of self-seeking. What's in it for me becomes the motto as we forget servant leadership and strive for personal greatness.

Remedy: Jesus' own model of ministry is compelling. As His disciples strove to climb, Jesus modeled the greatness of descent. Preach *Philippians* first to yourself and then preach it to your members.

Issue: **Overextension.** Face it. You will never accomplish all that you could and, seldom, all that you should. Pastoral work is never done. The reality of leadership is that someone will always need to be led. You'll destroy your leadership by concentrating on endless urgencies while ignoring the really important matters.

Remedy: Balance and prioritization. Determine what you can accomplish and then pursue excellence there without becoming sidetracked by urgent matters of less importance.

Issue: **Exclusivity.** No one ever resents the "in crowd" until they are excluded. Avoid the trap of associating with and listening only to those who comprise your inner circle. Ministry is compromised to the extent that anyone believes they are shut out.

Remedy: Become a mentor. Share the magic. Seek those who can be recruited and trained for service. Model ministry until they become effective and then encourage them to mentor others.

Issue: **Cronyism.** Job criteria should never be one's previous or current proximity to the leader. Committees that are staffed with only your buddies will soon be full of detractors. Nothing destroys creativity more quickly than compliant agreement.

Remedy: Listen to those with alternate views. Solicit input from those who are critical. Hire staff who are strong in your weak areas. Elect those who ask challenging questions. Encourage term limits.

Issue: **Lack of common sense.** *The Washington Post* newspaper advertises itself by proclaiming, "If you don't get it, you don't get it!" So it is with leadership and common sense. Nothing compensates for simple practicality. Too many leaders chase the impossible right past hundreds of opportunities to accomplish the possible.

Remedy: Ask yourself, will it work? Seek counsel. Refuse to elevate stupidity to a virtue. Chances are that if trusted counselors see no wisdom in a plan, it will not succeed just because it took root in your mind and you doggedly pursued it. Expect scrutiny of any idea.

Issue: **Failure to integrate faith and life.** A professional member of my last congregation consistently emphasized ministry in the workplace. Her message was clear. If my belief does not impact performance of my vocation, I am not a believer.

Remedy: Experience, then teach the impact of the gospel in your daily life and work.

[1] Special thanks to Bert Beach, Ray Dabrowski, Ben Maxson, Rose Otis, and Dick Stenbakken for sharing their wisdom.

WORSHIP IS A VERB

"And worship Him who made heaven and earth, the sea, and the fountains of water." — Revelation 14:7

As a people who understand the importance of worship in the prophetic context of last-day issues, it is disturbing to note the casual, humdrum manner with which too many congregations approach worshipful interaction with the Creator.

Can we really commemorate Christ's creative and redemptive activity with services that stifle participation, perpetuate the ordinary, and elevate repetition to the level of dogma?

Uninvolved and lacking experiential participation, our members vote with their feet to such an extent that in some countries we feel fortunate if more than half manage to attend one weekly service. Even the angels must struggle to stay awake.

Is it possible that we have spent so much time identifying the correct day and proclaiming the appropriate theology of sabbath keeping that we have missed actual worshiping? Have we become so concerned with the correctness of when we go to church that what we do when we get there no longer matters?

Flexible patterns. Many congregations are not flexible enough in their worship services to attract those who do not attend. As a result, these churches continue to decline. Others rush to judgment against those who do things differently. In fact, too often we confuse form with function and conclude that if others don't enjoy the same things we enjoy, then something is wrong with them; they must be either bad or mad.

Some congregations have split over worship style. Members who once fellowshipped together will hardly speak to those who hold a different opinion. Some invest such terror into a good biblical word, such as "celebrate," that others fear even to appear joyful. This need not be.

So how do we deal with a topic that is so potentially explosive? Should there be a uniquely Adventist experience when we worship? Does our theology impact our corporate expression of adoration and praise, or are we lethargically repeating traditions?

The early Christians typically worshiped in homes. The worship style of early Advent believers was quite expressive, nearly Pentecostal in nature. Our typical order of worship today is neither biblical nor Adventist.

Instead we follow a nineteenth-century style that relegates worship roles to platform leaders and a spectator role to the congregation. Much like a football game, in which thousands of spectators who desparately need exercise sit in the grandstand watching a few players who desparately need rest, our services have become spectator events. There is little active, participatory involvement of each worshiper with the Creator. The dynamic and vital encounter between Creator-God and worshiping penitent is too often absent.

Worship and church growth

Renewal of experiential worship can positively affect church growth as well as community outreach. Our previous congregation doubled its attendance in a relatively short period of time. Revitalized worship was an important contributing factor.

Believing that worship is a verb, we combined two words, "creative" and "active," to form our approach—"creactive"! Rather than a radically different format, our services became dynamically traditional. Attendees immediately recognized a typical Adventist service, but with a participative vitality. Guests and members experienced the old-shoe comfortability of the familiar, yet they often remarked that their worship experience was alive because they were involved.

We focused on attracting nonattenders. We included familiar and easy-to-sing hymns as well as more special musical presentations, even adding 15 minutes to the length of the service. We limited announcements, increased audience participation (Scripture reading, prayer requests, and testimonies), and provided sermon outlines in which hearers could "fill in the blanks."

We turned routine events such as child dedication, graduations, or service recognition into features which attracted the attendance of our members' extended family and friends for these occasions. Often these same friends and family became regular attendees and, ultimately, members.

Yes, worship is a verb. We as pastors must lead our congregations into creatively experiencing worship rather than merely observing!

For spiritual growth, *doing* is more important than *watching*!

HOW DO YOU
HANDLE TRUTH?

"Study to show thyself approved unto God,
a workman that needeth not to be ashamed,
rightly dividing the word of truth." — 2 Timothy 2:15

When desiring to encourage, or even to mandate, increased Scripture study, pastors and evangelists everywhere have utilized Paul's admonition to the young minister.

With typical proof-text fervency, we have used the text as an imperative to require Bible study in terminology that almost says "saved by the work of study" in order to gain God's approval.

While I have no doubt that God approves of Bible study and uses this process as the primary method of communicating His will to humanity today, I am convinced that this text has greater implications than merely stressing the requirement of scriptural study.

Without diminishing a commitment to encouraging both members and potential converts to study, or my conviction that God does, indeed, approve of studying His Word, the greater issue requires much more of me.

The initial, easier reading compliments me for orthodoxy—rightly dividing the word of truth. The second, more challenging, reading requires me to journey into the depths of my own soul—to ask how the truth has impacted my life and to apply the searchlight of Scripture to my own personal life.

Does God approve? Removed from the easier imperative to measure time spent in study, this question inquires as to whether my study has impacted my behavior. Can I measure my actions, my motives, my accomplishments, and my attempts on the scale of God's approval? Can I honestly face the query "Does God approve?" regarding my own behavior?

One of the greatest applications of this principle is the theme of Charles Sheldon's *In His Steps*. In this classic, members of a congregation purpose, before embarking upon any action, to ask themselves the question "What would Jesus do?" Then, as the story unfolds, the radical claims of the gospel affect their personal actions, choices, and behavior.

This is our need as spiritual leaders today. Personally, I need daily to ask, "What would Jesus do?" As I meet individuals I should first determine how Jesus would respond. His example should be my guide in treating others. Personally, I've discovered that determining that which God approves is not the difficult task. The demanding responsibility means that when asking if God approves, I must act in harmony with the conclusion.

Too often, I am tempted to want God's endorsement more than His approval. My temptation is to pray for the success of my ventures rather than to risk changing my plans based on the hard conclusion of determining God's approval.

Am I ashamed? When the apostle spoke of an unashamed workman, he had experienced the reality of his assertion. The quality of Paul's workmanship as a maker of tents determined his financial success. Prospective purchasers would tug the seams and test the stitching of Paul's products. Not only the immediate sale but his long-term reputation stood or fell on this inspection.

Can my work withstand closer inspection? Would I be ashamed for someone to know the shortcuts I take or the opportunities I skip? Would my behavior withstand scrutiny by One who understands my motives as well as my actions?

Is it the truth? Is the truth rightly handled? Rightly dividing the Word means more than correctly parsing the original language. The admonishment to leaders is to be someone "who correctly handles the word of truth."

First, of course, I have the responsibility to make certain my proclamation is accurate. My assertions must be based on God's Word and must reflect God's intent. Proof-texting my way to conclusions which I wish to confirm might appear to be based on the Word but fail to reveal the intent of Scripture.

Courts of justice expect witnesses to tell the truth, the whole truth, and nothing but the truth. It is not sufficient just to tell the truth partially. Teachers of the Word must tell the whole truth, and the implication of "nothing but the truth" means their testimony must not be compromised by half-truths or crucial evidence that has been withheld. No wonder the same apostle, Paul, warns that not all should seek to become religious instructors.

Beyond accuracy, however, I have a further responsibility to handle the truth carefully. A member once approached me with his concerns about the life of a fellow parishioner. He spoke the truth. There was no doubt about the accuracy of his assertions. But he failed the larger responsibility to speak the truth in love! In fact, the most unloving thing possible was to broadcast the truth of which he was so certain.

Scriptural study, if anything, must impact my relationship with Jesus and His creation in real-life daily existence. Hermeneutics confined to academia are dangerous; liberated in service, they are beautiful, life-filled, and life-giving.

In life, as well as hermeneutics, when tempted to seek the easier course of proof-text answers, it is vital to remember that the gospel's challenge is to seek heaven's more demanding, in-depth intent behind my initial reaction.

RESTORATION REQUIRES
REFORMATION

No doubt he would have gone far if he had not gone bad. He had unlimited potential, except for the tragedy he inflicted upon himself.

Humble origins were betrayed by high-octane ambitions. He grew up in a humid little backwater, a couple of hours' drive from the tropical coastal city where every aspiring fellow hoped his ship would come in. Townspeople back home considered him the local success story—until he went astray.

Of course his career didn't start out bad. He was somewhat different than the usual, but on the fast track to success. He eagerly grasped the fame and wealth that one can expect with outstanding talent.

After all, when he evaluated the lethargy of lesser competitors, it was easy to reason that he was worth all the extra money he paid himself beyond reasonable wages. He was unique, and others would soon discover his importance.

As for those who failed to affirm his valuable labors, he would curse them or resort to force to obtain his objectives.

As a son of prominence in his small hometown, the embarrassment was keen when he turned away from his family's tradition of selfless service.

It was particularly painful when he criticized those who remained within the framework of traditional experience as being indolent, self-content, and self-satisfied. He damned them as gluttons even as he robbed them. Arrogance was exceeded only by greed.

But what's this? Now he seeks restoration.

Now, parading across the same bridge he had tried to burn down, he says he again wants the faith of his father. Now he wants to feel the warm embrace of the group he has so viciously attacked and robbed. He wants acceptance and eagerly seeks reinstatement into the society whose doors he had slammed shut against himself.

This is not his first time to demand reestablishment in his former spiritual community. In fact, on several occasions his rituals of self-reform have sparked skepticism. Time after time he has proved his critics correct. Again and again he has disappointed those who hoped his conversion might be kosher. In fact, these repeated failures have confirmed their concept of him as being—incorrigible.

So what would make the difference this time? How can anyone certify this change as the real thing? What sets this latest episode apart from the opportunistic ventures that have grown out of his previous crusades to make things right with his family, his church, and his community?

He still resides in the luxurious house bought with funds stolen from those who trusted him most. He still operates his business as the same entrepreneurial genius he has prided himself to be. He still plies his trade and seeks to renovate his own kingdom even as he pursues restoration to the kingdom of grace.

So how could anyone trust this time to be different than all the others? The answer lies in that cryptic statement of Jesus, the teacher from Nazareth: "Therefore by their fruits you will know them" (Matt. 7:20).

"There is no evidence of genuine repentance unless it works reformation. If he restore the pledge, give again that he had robbed, confess his sins, . . . such were the effects that in former years followed seasons of religious awakening. Judged by their fruits, they were known to be blessed of God in the salvation of men and the uplifting of humanity."[1]

Interesting statement. Penetrating insight. Conversion will be evidenced by fruit. The result of new life in Christ is a new life in the community. Lip service is real if and only if words are backed up with action. To talk the talk, you must walk the walk. Restoration follows reformation.

No wonder the converted thief Zacchaeus publicly announces, "Here and now I give half of my possessions to the poor, and if I have cheated anybody out of anything, I will pay back four times the amount" (Luke 19:8, NIV).

No excuses! No posturing! No playing to the crowd! No papering over past misbehavior with protests of good intentions. Plain and simple, reformation means restoration—four times over for Zacchaeus.

So it is. Genuine conversion is confirmed by genuine restoration. If this means impoverishing himself or divesting himself of all he possesses, the reformed thief will recompense his victims.

Perhaps he cannot reclaim malicious words spoken, but he can surely repay looted lucre. Jesus works the miracle of salvation, and Zacchaeus responds with the miracle of restoration times four.

Jesus was right! By their fruits you shall know them. The fruits of the Spirit are evidenced by Spirit-filled responses.

Not a bad example for those seeking restoration today!

[1] Ellen G. White, *The Great Controversy* (Nampa, Idaho: Pacific Press Publishing Association, 1888), pp. 462, 463.

WHILE WE WAIT

I've got to show you something, pastor," Joe exclaimed as he unrolled a long strip of paper across my desk. On it he'd drawn an elaborate time line of prophetic events, from ancient times to the present and well into the future.

With a pen as a pointer, Joe eagerly traced a line right to the end of the chart, trying to interest me in some new innovation on an end-time event that he had just discovered in a little-referenced passage. In spite of my admiration for his artistic and eschatological diligence, I confess that it was only a moment before my eyes glazed over.

Joe must have noticed my loss of interest because suddenly he grasped my arm and said, "Pastor, these are things we absolutely must know if we're going to be ready for Jesus to come." Was Joe correct? Is this what it means to be ready for Jesus to return?

The essential message. As we commemorate the turning of the millennium with renewed hope and focus in the coming of Jesus, we must recognize the bad news—we are still here. After all, shouldn't we have been in the kingdom "long ere this"?

Ministry's first editor, L. E. Froom, understood that the vital issue is the message of Christ's coming more than its timing. In the inaugural issue he wrote, "The most irresistible thing in the world is a movement and a message whose time has come."

Froom then cited great movements and messages of spiritual history: Noah, Moses, John the Baptist, Jesus, Pentecost, the Reformation, and the Advent awakening. He concludes by saying of these movements, "They came each and all, in the will and providence of God, at the time appointed."

What is that message? Froom said, "Righteousness by faith is not a slogan or a catch phrase. It is not merely a doctrine to receive mental assent. It is a living experience that must become a personal actuality in all who shall triumph.... Call it what you will—the message of the indwelling Christ, the latter rain, genuine Christian experience, the deeper life, the victorious life, righteousness through Christ, the power of the Holy Spirit—if rightly understood, these are simply varying expressions for the one all-essential, crowning provision to prepare a people to meet their God. It is God's final call for an experimental fitness for translation day. . . . And let us remember continually the irresistibility of heaven-born principle set free at God's appointed time."

There it is. The question is not whether we are waiting for Jesus' return but how we are waiting. Our challenge is to do what we should at God's appointed time rather than to expend our energies in calculating dates and signs.

Relearning the lesson. Ironically, the very first lesson God taught Advent believers was that they were not to become too entranced with the timing of Christ's coming. In 1844 our pioneers predicted the date of the Second Advent and were disappointed. Right then and there they decided that Adventists would always eagerly await Jesus' return but they would never again specify when they expected it to happen.

This is a lesson we must continually relearn. For even if we don't set precise dates, we tend to let eschatological details captivate us as we eagerly follow purveyors of speculation.

Thinking to apply Jesus' counsel to watch and wait, some draw charts and do fascinating things with Bible numbers. Some look for esoteric bits of knowledge in out-of-the-way passages while others concentrate on political events and read great portent into every headline. Others study each move of other religious organizations as if this will reveal the secret.

My encounter with my overanxious church member compelled me to pen a limerick. Its message is better than its poetic depth:

> *A young theologian named Joe*
> *Eschatologically was "in the know,"*
> > *So he plotted and charted,*
> > *But the saints all departed*
> *While Joe had three signs yet to go.*

Do we prepare for the coming by merely "making a list and checking it twice"? Can we face the challenge of waiting while avoiding the pitfall of dictating the details to Deity?

I once took a photograph of my wife on a busy Hong Kong street. I must have stood a bit too far away from her, though, because when I saw the developed picture, I could hardly find Sharon amidst the cluttered background. The scene was so busy with people, cars, buildings, and signs that Sharon disappeared into the details.

When we fill our spiritual lives with the details of the Advent, the Lord of the Advent may well disappear into the background. Satan delights in sidetracking us.

Far too many view the great controversy as if the enemy controls the agenda. With sadness I observe some believers as more diligent about keeping an eye on the beast than they are about keeping their eyes on Jesus. They fail to emphasize beauty instead of the beast. Remember, Beauty wins! God wins in God's time!

The "how" of waiting. There is a better way to wait for Jesus to come. Matthew 24 pictures Jesus on the Mount of Olives. There, gazing down at the temple shining brilliant in the sunlight, He tells the disciples about the events that will happen before His return and warns them to watch and wait.

But knowing that what He says may be misunderstood, Jesus adds a parable. Imagine a small businessman putting his servant in charge of his affairs while he goes on a trip. But the boss's return is delayed. If this master has a bad servant, upon returning, he might find that the servant has given up waiting, spent his time "goofing off," or has even begun to fight with his fellow servants.

And what would the master find a good servant doing? Working. That's all! Simply doing the work the master wants him to do.

That's what it means to watch and wait. Faithful servants work while they wait for their Master to come home.

As they wait, they will be doing His business—preaching the gospel, helping those in need, raising good families, living Christian lives, winning souls to Christ—not speculating about dates and times.

Speculation versus faith. As the millennium approaches, some—even a few well-known names in our church—have stepped forth to declare that they have studied these details more diligently than the rest of us and can tell us, if not the day or hour, at least the general time of Christ's coming.

But while such tactics sell books, the popularity of these theories is not a good sign for Adventism. It suggests that even after 150 years we have never quite given up our desire to second-guess God. This is toxic religion at its extreme and defies the very words of our Lord, who said, "No man knows the day nor the hour."

Through the years, I have noticed that each time we Adventists have preoccupied ourselves with attempting to divine what will happen next, we lose spiritual perspective. We begin to "goof off," to scrap with one another about details, and to lose sight of both the Lord and His priorities.

I fear that We can become so preoccupied with coming events that we miss the coming King!

But when we have studied past events to see how the Lord has led us in accordance with His prophecies, our faith has been strengthened.

Why, then, you may ask, were these signs given, if not to provide us clues?

Nowhere does Jesus say, "I'm telling you these things so you can figure out what is going to happen next before everyone else does." If that is what He intended to do, it would contradict His advice about being ever ready and vigilant because "the day of the Lord will come as a thief in the night."

Jesus does say "I have told you now before it happens, so that when it does happen you will believe" (John 14:29).

Being ready. I earnestly want Jesus to return. And I quite agree with Joe that we are not ready. But this is not because we have failed to memorize his time line. It is because we have failed to experience Jesus' other advent. There is, you see, an advent of Christ in between the one recorded in the gospels and the one described in Revelation.

The vital coming between Bethlehem and Armageddon is when Jesus comes into our hearts right now. And unless Christ has first been invited to come into the hearts and lives of His people, He will never come for us in the heavens.

If our Lord delays His coming, it is not because we have failed to trace out the right chart, calculate the right formula, or spot the right portentous event. It is because we have been too busy tracing, calculating, and spotting to welcome and know our life-changing Lord Himself.

Editor Froom was correct in understanding the primacy of righteousness by faith—faith in Jesus and His righteousness that enlivens, transforms, and, ultimately, translates God's people.

What will the Lord find you doing when He returns?

MARY K. AND
KARLA FAYE

These two women could not have been more different. Mary K. was a woman of virtue. Karla Faye was a woman of violence.

For nearly sixty years, Mary K. gave her life in willing service to others. During her much shorter life, Karla Faye destroyed the lives of others.

Recently, much of the world watched and waited to see if Karla Faye Tucker would become the first woman executed by the state of Texas in 135 years. Thousands of individuals, including personal pleas to the governor from such notables as Pope John Paul II and Pat Robertson, prayed that her life would be spared from the lethal injection which finally ended her life.

Now let's make one thing clear. Karla Faye Tucker deserved to die for her sins.

Back in 1983, during a weekend orgy with her boyfriend, Karla Faye, a drug-addicted prostitute, consumed astonishing quantities of Valium, heroin, speed, percodan, mandrax, marijuana, dialudid, methadone, tequila, and rum. Then, in a revenge robbery, the pair brutally murdered two individuals by hacking their bodies into pieces with a pickax.

A Texas jury found the evidence of her guilt so compelling and her crime so heinous, they sentenced Karla Faye to death for her deeds.

And at the end, Karla Fay received the penalty she deserved, despite unmistakable evidence that while in prison she had been genuinely converted and had become a born-again Christian.

Neither legal appeals that reached even the U.S. Supreme Court, nor earnest requests for mercy by famous preachers, nor a United Nations resolution, nor the fervent prayers of thousands of believers, deterred her execution from moving ahead on schedule.

Of course, not everyone prayed for Karla Faye's life to be spared. Although the brother of one of her victims pled for her death sentence to be commuted, the husband of that same victim expressed his delight in the approaching death penalty and loudly declared that Karla was about to meet his wife "on the other side." There, he asserted, she would receive an even more severe punishment.

Likewise, skeptics of jailhouse conversions declared that any prisoner facing execution will get religion and that if Karla Faye's conversion was not "death bed," it was, at the very least, "death row." They pointed out that jailhouse conversions are both commonplace and irrelevant in deciding who gets a reprieve and that Texas has never granted pardon to anyone based on a religious conversion.

On the other hand, Mary K. was the consummate pastor's wife. Baptized as a young girl of 14, she devotedly followed her Lord for the next 56 years, over half a century of that in partnership ministry.

If Mary K. understood God's will on any subject, she followed it. All who knew her declared she was a saint, if for no other reason than that she faithfully supported her pastor spouse, who acknowledges he was "difficult" to live with.

Throughout their ministry, Mary K. was often the oil poured on troubled waters in the churches they served, and her sweet spirit was influential in showing many the meaning of God's love.

From a young age, Mary K. dedicated all the talents which she possessed to Christ's service. Her musical abilities, organizational skills, outgoing demeanor, savvy understanding of personalities, intuitive comprehension, firm will, and financial acumen consistently secured the best for God's cause and for her family.

As a direct result of her influence, each of Mary K's three sons became ministers. The Biblical description of a virtuous woman aptly describes her life.

Finally, facing her threescore and tenth birthday in declining health, Mary K. expressed her confidence in her Saviour and her desire to rest in Jesus rather than to continue the struggle with pain and disability. In His mercy, our Heavenly Father allowed her to fall asleep in Jesus.

Now let's make one more thing clear. Mary K. deserved to die for her sins.

You may wonder at this assertion after I've told you of her saintly service through so many decades. But the reality is that Mary K. was as much a sinner as Karla Faye.

Scripture declares the wages of sin is death, and, like Karla Faye, Mary K. was a sinner. Whether pastor's spouse or pickax prostitute, the reality of human existence is that we are sinners. We may all sin differently, but we are all alike sinners.

I can even tell you a few of Mary K.'s faults. Although she would have never stooped to their level, she seldom suffered fools or their ventures. She also made obedience a virtue to the extent that she later realized she had never fully known the reality of righteousness by faith until the last decade of her life when she read the personal testimony of Martin Weber in his book *My Tortured Conscience* and experienced years of greater joy as a result.

Now Mary K. was several decades ahead of Karla Faye in her walk with God as well as light-years ahead in the process of sanctification, the lifelong, ongoing experience of God's work in the lives of His people.

But in the assurance of justification and in eager anticipation of resurrection, the pastor's wife was not one step ahead of the pickax killer.

Although they approached their deaths from different perspectives, both these women now await the promised resurrection when Jesus returns.

Both Mary K. and Karla Faye approached death in the certainty of the blessed hope. Mary K. knew that she would experience the rest of the blessed in Jesus, and Karla Faye was certain that she would meet Jesus face-to-face the next moment after her execution.

And that blessed hope they shared is the personal promise of our Saviour. *If I go to prepare a place for you, I will come again, to receive you unto myself that where I am, there you may be also (John 14:1-3).*

The whole purpose of Jesus' return is to reunite Himself with His people so that we can all be together in His kingdom.

Blessed hope! Blessed assurance!

Behold, I show you a mystery. We shall not all sleep, but we shall all be changed. In a moment, in the twinkling of an eye, at the last trump. For the trumpet shall sound and the dead shall be raised incorruptible and we shall be changed. For this corruptible must put on incorruption, and this mortal must put on immortality.

So when this corruptible shall have put on incorruption, and this mortal shall have put on immortality, then shall be brought to pass the saying that is written, death is swallowed up in victory (1 Corinthians 15:51-54).

For the Lord Himself shall descend from heaven with a shout, with the voice of the archangel, with the trump of God and the dead in Christ shall rise first. Then, we which are alive and remain shall be caught up together with them in the clouds to meet the Lord in the air and so shall we ever be with the Lord. Wherefore comfort one another with these words (1 Thessalonians 4:16-18).

By the way, I share the blessed hope with Mary K. and Karla Faye. In fact, I am personally related to these two women of such disparate backgrounds.

Mary K. Cress is my mother. And Karla Faye Tucker, through our mutual faith in Jesus, is my sister.